Starter

John Stevens

Beratende Mitarbeit

Astrid Hornoff, Leipzig
Christine House, Berlin
Isobel Williams, Freiburg

Englisch
für
Erwachsene

First Choice

Cornelsen

Welcome!

Herzlich willkommen bei *First Choice Starter*!

Wenn Sie noch nie Englisch gelernt haben, oder aber lieber noch einmal ganz von vorne anfangen möchten, weil Sie das Meiste vergessen haben, ist *First Choice Starter* das richtige Lehrwerk für Sie.

In einem angemessenen Lerntempo erwerben Sie Schritt für Schritt die sprachlichen Grundlagen, um sich mit anderen über Familie, Alltag und Freizeit zu unterhalten. Sie bauen einen Grundwortschatz auf und meistern die Anfänge der englischen Grammatik. So wird nach und nach eine solide Basis für das Weiterlernen geschaffen. Außerdem erhalten Sie viele Tipps für das Erlernen einer Fremdsprache, bei denen auch der Spaß am Lernen nicht zu kurz kommt.

Wo finde ich was?

Ihr Kursbuch hat folgende Bestandteile:

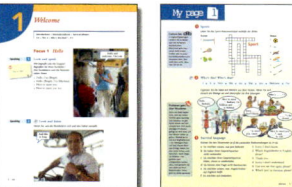

- acht *Units*, die Sie im Unterricht mit Ihrem Kursleiter / Ihrer Kursleiterin bearbeiten. In diesen Units steht das Sprechen im Vordergrund.

- Am Ende jeder Unit finden Sie immer eine Seite (*My page* = Meine Seite), mit der Sie das in der Kursstunde Gelernte zu Hause weiter üben und festigen können.

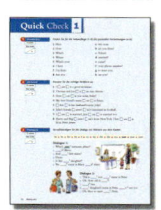

- ein *I can*-Abschnitt am Ende jeder Unit zur Bewertung Ihres Lernfortschritts in Anlehnung an die Vorgaben des *CEF*.

- zwei *Quick Check* Wiederholungseinheiten (nach den Units 4 und 8). Hier können Sie Ihren Lernstand überprüfen.

- einen Anhang mit einer *Grammatikübersicht*, dem Lösungsschlüssel zu den *My page*-Übungen und den *Quick Checks* sowie den *Transcripts*, d.h. den Texten zu den Hörverständnis-Übungen.

- ein *Phrasebook* mit allen Wörtern und Wendungen aus dem Kursbuch zum Lernen und Nachschlagen. Dieses Buch eignet sich auch zum Lernen und Wiederholen unterwegs. Es enthält auch eine Liste der geographischen Begriffe.

- ein Lesezeichen mit nützlichen Wendungen zum Nachfragen und für das Gespräch im Unterricht sowie

- eine CD mit allen Hörverständnis-Übungen aus dem Kursbuch.

Viel Spaß im Englischkurs und viel Erfolg wünschen Ihnen Autorenteam und Redaktion!

Table of contents

GRAMMAR	FUNCTIONS & SITUATIONS	MINI-TASKS
I'm; This is; Who's this/that?; It's	Introductions	Make word groups
I, you, he, she; am, are, is; What's … ; genitive *'s; my, your, his, her*	Meeting & greeting Talking about where you are from	Make a class list Make a picture quiz
Questions & short answers with *be*; plural of nouns; articles *a, an, the*	Asking for & giving personal details	Find someone who … Complete your class list
The simple present (1); statements and questions	Talking about likes & dislikes	Make a class profile
The simple present (2); *they're – their*	Talking about your family	Find out more about someone's family
Prepositions of time	Asking & telling the time	Write a quiz
Simple present with time adverbials	Describing your daily/weekly routine	Make a timeline
Time adverbials with *every; there is; can/can't*	Describing where you live	Make a mini-profile of your partner

1 *Welcome*

Introductions • Internationalisms • Survival phrases
I'm • This is • Who's this/that? • It's

Focus 1 *Hello*

Speaking | **1**

Look and speak.

Wie begrüßt Lola die Gruppe? Begrüßen Sie Ihren Kursleiter / Ihre Kursleiterin und die Personen neben Ihnen.

A Hello, I'm (Birgit).
B Hello, (Birgit). I'm (Martina).
A Nice to meet you.
B Nice to meet you too.

(!) I'm = I am

Hello and welcome. I'm Lola.

Speaking | **2**

02 Look and listen.

Hören Sie, wie die Reiseleiterin sich und den Fahrer vorstellt.

And this is Tony.

Now speak.

Stellen Sie die Personen neben Ihnen dem Kursleiter / der Kursleiterin vor.

A This is (Marek).
  And this is (Martina).
TEACHER Nice to meet you (Marek).
  And nice to meet you too, (Martina).

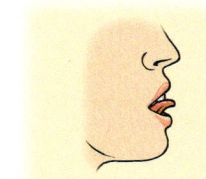

> (!) Zeigen Sie beim th ruhig mal Ihre Zunge!

Practice | **3** | ### Put in order.

Bringen Sie die Sätze in die richtige Reihenfolge.

__ A And this is Vanessa.
1 A Hello, I'm Mark.
__ B Hello, Vanessa. Nice to meet you too.
__ B Nice to meet you, Mark.

(03) **Now listen and check, then repeat.**

Hören Sie zu und überprüfen Sie Ihre Lösung. Dann sprechen Sie nach.

Speaking
Whole class | **4** | ### Walk and talk.

Gehen Sie in der Klasse umher und begrüßen Sie andere Kursmitglieder. Jedes Mal, wenn der Kursleiter / die Kursleiterin unterbricht, stellen Sie Ihren Gesprächspartner / Ihre Gesprächspartnerin dem Kursmitglied vor, das neben Ihnen steht.

Useful language

Hello, I'm …
And I'm …
Nice to meet you (too).
This is …

Speaking | **5** | ### Listen and answer.

Ihr Kursleiter / Ihre Kursleiterin überprüft nun die Namen. Beantworten Sie die Fragen. Danach fragen Sie Ihren Partner / Ihre Partnerin.

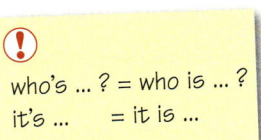

> (!) who's … ? = who is … ?
> it's … = it is …

TEACHER Who's this?
A It's (Birgit).
TEACHER And who's that?
B It's (Marek).
TEACHER And who's this?
C Sorry, I don't know.

Practice **6** **Look and listen.**

Pair work

Albert Einstein
Charlie Chaplin
President Kennedy
Marilyn Monroe
Steffi Graf
Bill Gates
Pope Benedict XVI

A Who's this?
B I think it's (Albert Einstein).
A No, it's not (Albert Einstein).
   I think it's (Charlie Chaplin).
   And this is (Charlie Chaplin) too.
B Yes, it's (Charlie Chaplin).

Look and speak.

Sehen Sie sich die Fotos an und identifizieren Sie die Prominenten.

Focus 2 *International words*

Pronunciation **7** **Listen and repeat.**

Hören Sie, wie diese Wörter auf Englisch ausgesprochen werden. Sprechen Sie nach.

> hamburger • hockey
> hotel • pilot • sandwich
> steak • volleyball

Mini-task **8** **Make word groups.**

Pair work

Hier sehen Sie englische Wörter, von denen Sie sicher einige kennen. Ordnen Sie die Wörter in das entsprechende Diagramm. Ergänzen Sie weitere Wörter, die Sie kennen.

> ~~airport~~ • ~~badminton~~ • check-in • cocktail • drink • hamburger
> hockey • hot dog • hotel • jogging • last minute • match
> pilot • pizza • sandwich • snack • snowboard • steak
> surfing • taxi • team • tennis • ticket • training • volleyball

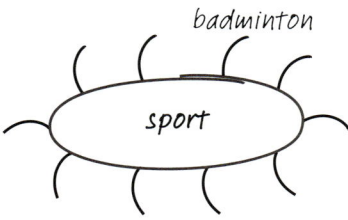

badminton

sport

food & drink

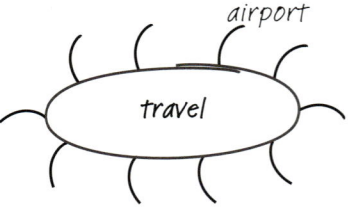

airport

travel

Focus 3 *Survival phrases*

Reading **9** **Look and read.**

Desmond lernt Deutsch. Sehen Sie sich den Cartoon an und lesen Sie die Sprechblasen.

06 **Now listen and repeat.**

Hören Sie sich die Wendungen im Kasten an und sprechen Sie nach.

What's *Bahnhof* in English, please?	*Wie heißt ,Bahnhof' auf Englisch, bitte?*
What's 'station' in German, please?	*Wie heißt station auf Deutsch, bitte?*
Can you say that again, please?	*Können Sie das bitte noch einmal sagen?*
Thank you.	*Danke.*
Sorry, I don't understand.	*Entschuldigung, ich verstehe nicht.*
Sorry, I don't know.	*Es tut mir Leid, ich weiß es nicht.*

Speaking **10** **Ask your teacher.**

Whole class

Finden Sie heraus, wie diese Gegenstände auf Englisch heißen und wie die englischen Wörter ausgesprochen werden. Verwenden Sie die Wendungen aus Übung 9.

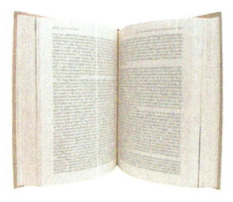

I can …

Bewerten Sie Ihren Lernerfolg. Ergänzen Sie.

Folgende Wörter, die ich gelernt habe, sind mir wichtig.

_____

_____

_____

_____

_____

Ich kann:
– *mich mit Namen vorstellen.*

   Hello, _____ .

– *sagen, dass ich mich freue, jemanden kennen zu lernen.*

   Nice _____ .

– *jemanden einer anderen Person vorstellen.*

   _____ *is Bernard.*

– *fragen, wer jemand ist, und darauf antworten.*

   _____ *'s that? – It's Anna.*

– *,bitte', ,danke' und ,Entschuldigung' sagen.*

   please – thank you – sorry _____

– *fragen, wie etwas auf Englisch heißt.*

   What's _____ *, please?*

– *nach der deutschen Übersetzung eines Wortes fragen.*

   _____ *, please?*

– *jemanden bitten, etwas zu wiederholen.*

   Can you _____ *, please?*

– *sagen, dass ich etwas nicht verstehe.*

   Sorry, I don't _____ .

– *sagen, dass ich etwas nicht weiß.*

   Sorry, I don't _____ .

1 Sports

Culture link 🔗

Lösen Sie das Sport-Kreuzworträtsel mithilfe der Bilder.

Culture link

In englischsprachigen Ländern ist es üblich, sich mit Vornamen anzusprechen. Manchmal geht man schon beim ersten Treffen oder in einer Geschäftssituation zum Vornamen über. Das heißt aber nicht, dass man *per du* ist.

Across

2
5
8

Down

1
3
4
6
7
9

Sport

07 2 Who's this? Who's that?

I ● It ● Nice ● this ● too ● that ● you ● Welcome ● I'm

Ergänzen Sie die Sätze mit Wörtern aus dem Kasten. Hören Sie sich danach die Dialoge an und überprüfen Sie Ihre Lösungen.

Probieren geht über Studieren

Wenn ein Baby laufen lernt, sind die ersten Schritte ganz wackelig und unsicher, es gibt kleine Stürze und viel Unsicherheit. Erst durch ständiges Probieren gelingt es dem Kind, auf zwei Beinen sicher zu gehen. Ähnlich ist es mit dem Englischlernen – nur ständiges Üben und sich Trauen führt zum Erfolg. Haben Sie also keine Scheu vorm Sprechen, keine Angst vor Fehlern – sie gehören zum erfolgreichen Lernen dazu. Und genieren Sie sich nicht vor Ihren Mitlernenden: ihnen geht es sicher genauso.

Hello. _____¹ Barbara.

Nice to meet _____², Barbara. I´m Andreas and _____³ is Helmut.

Who´s _____⁴?

Sorry, _____⁵ don't know.

_____⁶'s the clown!

_____⁷ to meet you, Laura.

Nice to meet you _____⁸, Jack. _____⁹ to CRS.

3 Survival language

Ordnen Sie den Situationen (a–f) die passenden Redewendungen zu (1–6).

a *Sie möchten wissen, was* pen *bedeutet.*

b *Sie haben Ihren Gesprächspartner nicht verstanden.*

c *Sie möchten Ihren Gesprächspartner bitten, etwas zu wiederholen.*

d *Sie können eine Frage nicht beantworten.*

e *Sie möchten wissen, was ‚Kugelschreiber'auf Englisch heißt.*

f *Sie möchten sich bedanken.*

1 Sorry, I don't know.

2 What's *Kugelschreiber* in English, please?

3 Thank you.

4 Sorry, I don't understand.

5 Can you say that again, please?

6 What's 'pen' in German, please?

2 *People & places*

Names • Country names
I, you, he, she • *am, are, is* • *What's …?* • genitive *'s* • *my, your, his, her*
Where are you from?

Focus 1 *Names*

Speaking

Whole class

1 **Look and speak.**

Begrüßen Sie noch einmal die anderen Kursmitglieder. Falls Sie einen Namen vergessen haben, fragen Sie wie im Bild.

⚠️ what's = what is

Hello again. → Hello. → Sorry, what's your name? → I'm (Marek).

Sorry, what's your name?

Speaking | **2** | (08) **Listen, read and complete.**

Hören und lesen Sie den Dialog. Ergänzen Sie die Sätze neben dem Foto.

RECEPTIONIST	Sorry, what's your name?
MAN	Grant.
RECEPTIONIST	Is that your surname?
MAN	Yes. My first name is Scott.
RECEPTIONIST	So you're Scott Grant.
MAN	That's right.

His first name is _____.
His surname is _____.

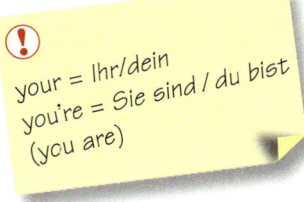

(!) your = lhr/dein
you're = Sie sind / du bist
(you are)

(09) **Now listen and repeat.**

Hören Sie zu und sprechen Sie nach.

Pre-task | **3** | (10) **Complete, then listen and check.**
Pair work

Vervollständigen Sie den Dialog mit den Wörtern im Kasten.

it's ● my ● what ● your ● you're

A _____'s^1 your name, please? A So _____^{5} Pat Lindsey.
B Lindsey.   B Yes, that's right.
A Is that _____^{2} first name?   A Can you write that, please?
B No, _____^{3} my surname.
  _____^{4} first name is Pat.

Read the dialogue with a partner.

Lesen Sie den Dialog mit einem anderen Kursmitglied.

Mini-task | **4** | **Make a class list.**
Whole class

Name	Phone number	Mobile number

Hinten im Buch finden Sie eine Vorlage für eine Namensliste. Stehen Sie auf, gehen Sie in der Klasse umher und fragen Sie die anderen Kursmitglieder nach ihren Vor- und Nachnamen.

Useful language

Sorry, what's your first name?
What's your surname, please?
So your name is … / So you're …
Yes, that's right.
Can you write that, please?

Focus 2 *Other people*

Reading **5** ## Read and complete.

Lesen Sie die Texte und vervollständigen Sie die Tabelle.

This is Pat Lindsey.
She's from England.
Pat's family is from London.
But she's married to an American.
Her husband is from New York.

This is Pat's business partner.
His name is Don Stewart.
He's from Scotland.
His family is from Glasgow.
Don's not married, he's single.

> (!) she's = she is
> he's = he is

First name	Surname	From	Family from	Married?
Pat	_____	_____	_____	_____
Don	_____	_____	_____	_____

(11) **Now listen and repeat.**

Hören Sie zu und sprechen Sie nach.

Grammar   ☞ p. 75

I'm (I am) Tony.   **My** surname is Marshall.
You're (You are) Don Stewart.   **Your** surname is Stewart.
He's (He is) from Scotland.   **His** family is from Glasgow.
She's (She is) from England.   **Her** name is Pat.

Practice **6** ## Read and decide.

Lesen Sie und kreuzen Sie das richtige Wort an.

1 ☐ He's   ☐ She's Pat Lindsey.
2 ☐ He's   ☐ His   first name is Don.
3 ☐ He's   ☐ His   Don Stewart.
4 ☐ She   ☐ Her   surname is Lindsey.
5 ☐ He's   ☐ His   from Glasgow.
6 ☐ She's ☐ He's   Pat's business partner.

> (!) He's Pat's partner.
> = He **is** Pat's partner.
> Er ist Pats Partner.

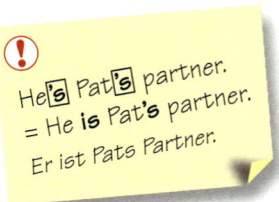

12 **Now listen and decide.**

Welches Wort hören Sie?

1 ☐ he's ☐ his   3 ☐ she's ☐ please

2 ☐ she's ☐ he's   4 ☐ his   ☐ this

Game

Whole class

7 **Listen and speak.**

Bilden Sie zwei Teams. Machen Sie Aussagen über Prominente. Kann das andere Team den Namen vervollständigen?

A His surname is Armstrong. → Louis? → No, sorry. Not Louis Armstrong. Lance Armstrong. → One point for Team A.

B Her first name is Julia. → Julia Roberts? → Right! → One point for Team A.

Practice

8 **Please complete: 's/is, 're/are, 'm/am.**

DON My name_____ Don. I_____ Don Stewart. That_____ a Scottish name.

I_____ Pat's business partner. She_____ in New York, and I_____ in London.

Pat_____ from London, but she_____ a New Yorker now.

PAT My office _____ in New York, and my husband _____ from New York.
But my family _____ from London.

_____ I a New Yorker, or a Londoner?

DON You_____ a New Yorker, a New Yorker from London.

PAT And you ____ a Londoner from Scotland.

Now complete: *What's his/her name?* and *Where's he/she from?*

TONY Your business partner in New York: ***what***_____ again?

DON Pat, Pat Lindsey.

TONY And ***where***_____ ?

DON Well, her family is from London.

PAT My husband is American.

TONY _____ ?

PAT New York. He's a New Yorker.

TONY And _____ ?

PAT Brad. That's an American name.

Focus 3 *Places*

Group work

9 ## Where is it?

Sehen Sie sich die Fotos an.
Wo befinden sich diese Orte?

Australia ● Britain ● Canada ● USA

San Francisco

Sydney

London

Toronto

New York

Ayer's Rock (Uluru)

13 **Now look, listen and repeat.**

Schauen Sie sich die Karte auf Seite 17 an, hören Sie zu und sprechen Sie nach.
Hören Sie sich danach die nächste Liste an und machen Sie einen Haken bei den
Ländernamen, die genannt werden.

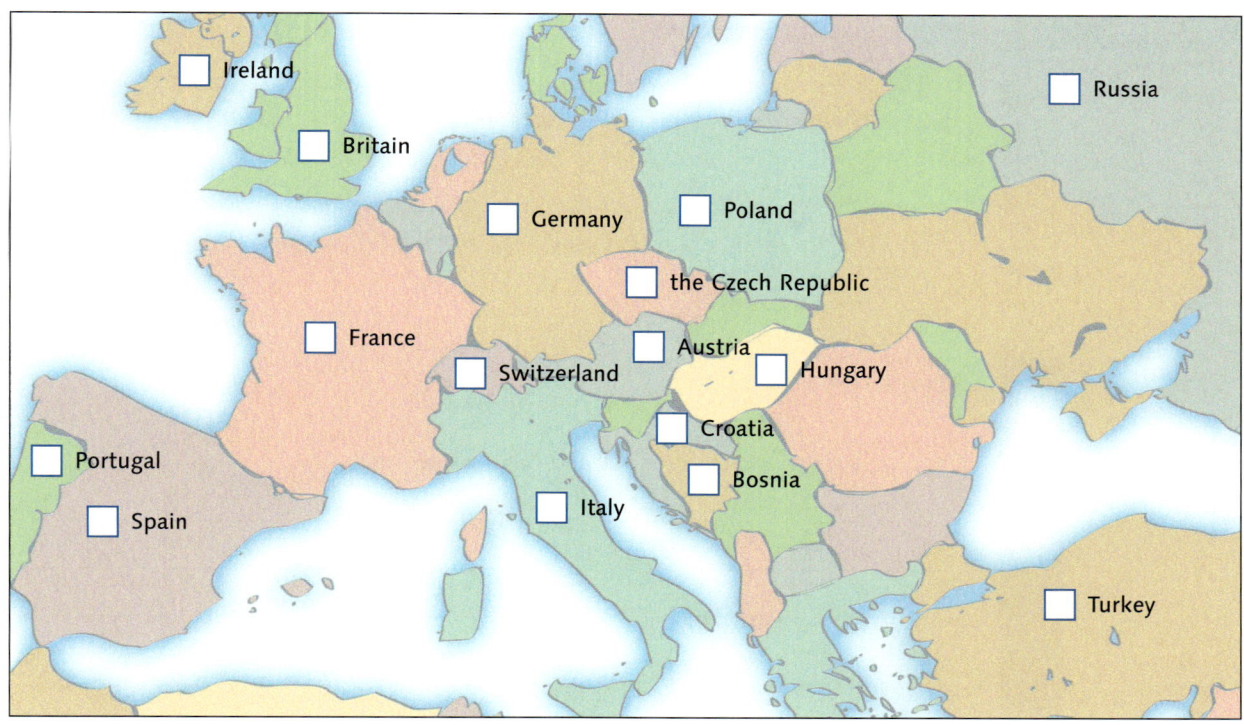

Ireland Russia Britain Germany Poland the Czech Republic France Austria Switzerland Hungary Croatia Portugal Bosnia Spain Italy Turkey

Speaking
Whole class

10 Look, then ask and answer.

Schauen Sie sich den Cartoon an. Befragen Sie sich danach gegenseitig.

Pre-task
Group work

11 Look and answer.

Welches Land ist hier gemeint?
Eine ausführliche Liste der Ländernamen finden
Sie im Phrasebook.

Useful language

This is England. Yes, OK.
No, I think it's (France). What's … in English?

Mini-task **12**
Group work

Make a picture quiz.

1 *Wählen Sie in Ihrer Arbeitsgruppe zwei Länder aus. Was assoziieren Sie mit diesen Ländern (Essen & Trinken, Orte, berühmte Personen, ...)? Zeichnen Sie zwei Bildergruppen wie in Übung 11.*

2 *Nun tauschen Sie Ihr Quiz mit dem einer anderen Gruppe. Finden Sie das gesuchte Land heraus und zeigen Sie es anschließend dem Kurs.*

I can ...

Bewerten Sie Ihren Lernerfolg. Ergänzen Sie.

Folgende Wörter, die ich gelernt habe, sind mir wichtig.

_____

_____

_____

Ich kann
– folgende Länder auf Englisch benennen.

_____

_____

_____

– jemanden nach seinem Namen fragen.

   What _____ *, please?*

– meinen eigenen Vor- und Nachnamen sagen.

   My _____ *.*

   And my _____ *.*

– etwas bestätigen und sagen, dass es richtig ist.

   Yes, that's _____ *.*

– jemanden bitten, etwas zu schreiben.

   Can _____ *, please?*

– sagen, wo ich herkomme.

   I'm _____ *.*

– jemanden fragen, wo er herkommt.

   Where _____ *?*

Außerdem kann ich Folgendes richtig anwenden:
• I am – you are – he is, she is, it is, this is, that is
• my – your – his – her
• besitzanzeigendes 's (Pat's partner)

My page 2

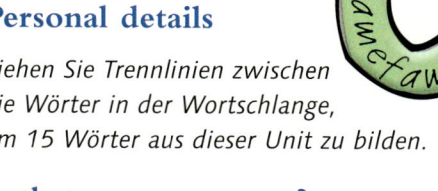

1 Personal details

Ziehen Sie Trennlinien zwischen die Wörter in der Wortschlange, um 15 Wörter aus dieser Unit zu bilden.

(14) 2 Is that your surname?

a *Setzen Sie die fehlenden Buchstaben ein. (Tipp: Die Wortschlange hilft Ihnen!)*

1 What's you _ na _ _ ?   3 I _ that y _ _ _ hu _ _ _ _ _ ?
2 What's yo _ _ su _ _ _ _ _ ?   4 Who _ _ that?

b *Ordnen Sie die Fragen den richtigen Antworten zu und hören Sie sich dann die Aufnahme an. Hatten Sie Recht?*

a Yes. His name's Olaf.   **c** Schmidt.
b That's my business partner, Heinrich, and his family.   **d** Lilo.

3 Where's she from?

Ergänzen Sie die Fragen zu Julie. Bilden Sie dann Fragen und die passenden Antworten zu Manfred Frey auf einem Extrablatt.

NAME: Julie Levant
FROM: France
FAMILY FROM: Paris
PARTNER: Tony Dimarco
FROM: Italy
FAMILY FROM: Rome

NAME: Manfred Frey
FROM: Switzerland
FAMILY FROM: Zürich
PARTNER: Marta Dubow
FROM: Hungary
FAMILY FROM: Budapest

he • her • his • she • What (×2) • Where (×4)

Questions	Answers
1 _____'s Julie's surname?	Levant.
2 _____'s _____ from?	France.
3 _____'s _____ family from?	Paris.
4 _____'s her partner's name?	Tony Dimarco.
5 _____'s _____ from?	Italy.
6 _____'s _____ family from?	Rome.

4 Places

Sortieren Sie die Buchstaben, so dass sie Ländernamen ergeben.

eht ecchz eiubclpr

aegmnry   eukrty   ainps   aouglprt   aiussr   aodlnp   aughnry   aaiocrt

3 Contacts

Greetings • Phone numbers • Talking about interests • Numbers 0–10
Questions & short answers with *be* • Plural of nouns
(Good) Morning • *How are you?* • articles *a, an* & *the*

Focus 1 *Greetings*

Songs **1** (15) **Listen and decide.**

Welche zwei der folgenden Wörter hören Sie in den beiden Liedern: morning,
afternoon, evening, night?

	morning	afternoon	evening	night
song 1	☐	☐	☐	☐
song 2	☐	☐	☐	☐

Welche Lieder kennen Sie, in denen einer oder mehrere der Begriffe vorkommen?

Reading **2**   **16** **Read, listen and complete.**

WAITER   _____ ¹.
WOMAN   Good _____ ².
WAITER   And how are you this morning?
WOMAN   Not so bad, thanks. And you?
WAITER   I'm fine, _____ ³.
        What's your room number, please?
WOMAN   607.

Now ask and answer.

A How are you this morning/afternoon/evening?
B _____, thanks. And you?
A _____, thanks.

Practice **3**   **17** **Listen and decide. (✔)**

❗
who?   = wer?
where? = wo?

1 ☐ who   ☐ how
2 ☐ who   ☐ where
3 ☐ what   ☐ that
4 ☐ where   ☐ her

Now complete: *how, what, where, who.*

1 _____ are you from? – I'm from Germany.

2 _____ are you this evening? – Fine, thanks.

3 _____'s that? – Monica. She's my business partner.

4 _____'s her surname? – Baxter.

Pronunciation **4**   **18** **Listen and repeat.**

❗
w: wie ein ganz
kurzes u – aber mit
gestülpten Lippen!

what
where
Washington
S**w**itzerland

w

Focus 2 *Numbers 0–10*

Speaking **5** ### Read and answer. What is the number?

Um welche Zahl handelt es sich?

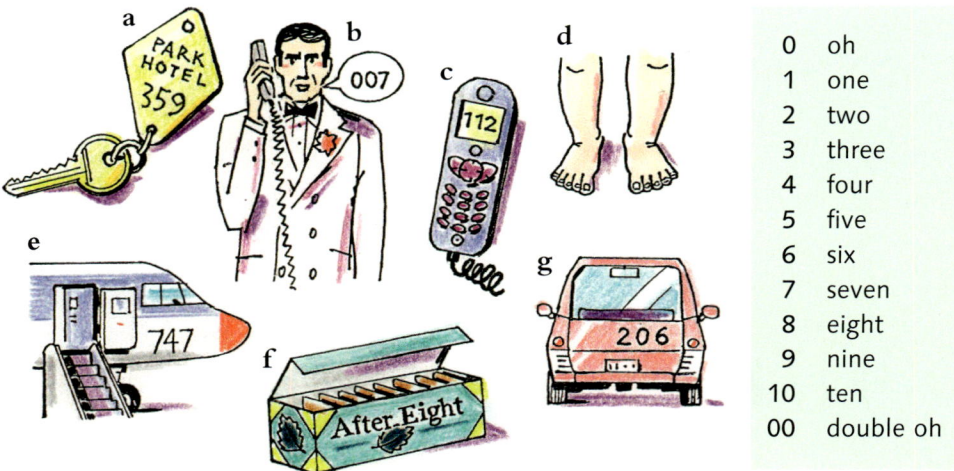

0	oh
1	one
2	two
3	three
4	four
5	five
6	six
7	seven
8	eight
9	nine
10	ten
00	double oh

Pre-task **6** ### Ask and answer with your teacher, then with a partner.

Beantworten Sie die Fragen zusammen mit Ihrem Kursleiter / Ihrer Kursleiterin. Fragen Sie dann ein anderes Kursmitglied.

TEACHER What's your phone number, please?

A _____.

TEACHER Thanks.
And what's your mobile number?

A _____.

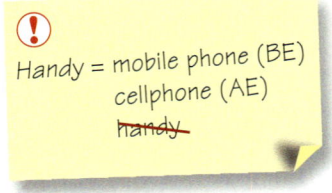

mobile phone

Pair work ### Now write three phone numbers, then dictate the numbers to your partner.

Schreiben Sie jetzt drei Telefonnummern auf und diktieren Sie sie anschließend Ihrem Partner / Ihrer Partnerin.

(!) Handy = mobile phone (BE) cellphone (AE) ~~handy~~

Mini-task **7** **Complete your class list.**

Whole class

Name	Phone number	Mobile number

Ergänzen Sie die Liste am Ende Ihres Buches. Stehen Sie auf und gehen Sie in der Klasse umher. Fragen Sie die anderen Kursmitglieder und ergänzen Sie die Einträge in der Liste.

Useful language

What's your name again, please?
What's your phone number, please?
And what's your mobile number?
Sorry, can you say that again, please?
I don't have a mobile.
Sorry, I don't know my number.

Focus 3 *Interests*

Vocabulary **8** **Please complete.**

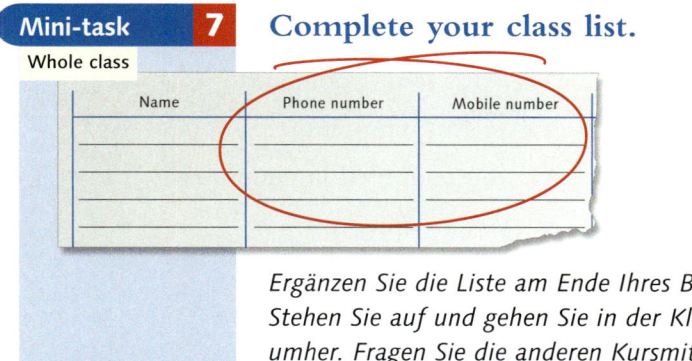

an internet user

an opera singer

a good cook

a taxi driver

a football fan

1 *A football fan*_____ is interested in sport.

2 _____ is interested in music.

3 _____ is interested in food.

4 _____ is interested in computers.

5 _____ is or is not interested in cars.

Grammar ☞ p. 74

a fan, **an** opera fan
the [ðə] fan,
the [ðɪ] opera fan

a cook, two cook**s**
a fan, two fan**s**

Pronunciation **9** (19) **Listen, then listen and repeat.**

What's your name? Are you a good cook?

Where are you from? Are you an internet user?

Who's that? Are you interested in computers?

How are you? Are you an opera fan?

Speaking **10** **Ask your teacher.**

		Yes	No
1	Are you a good cook?	☐	☐
2	Are you interested in cars?	☐	☐
3	Are you an internet user?	☐	☐
4	Are you interested in computers?	☐	☐
5	Are you interested in sport?	☐	☐
6	Are you a good swimmer?	☐	☐
7	Are you interested in pop music?	☐	☐
8	Are you a coffee drinker?	☐	☐

(!) isn't = is not

Grammar

☞ p. 75

Are you a good cook? Yes, **I am**. // No, **I'm not**.

Is he a good cook? Yes, **he is**. // No, **he's not**. / No, **he isn't**.

Is she a good cook? Yes, **she is**. // No, **she's not**. / No, **she isn't**.

Practice **11** **Please complete.**

1 A _____ you interested in sport?

B No, I_____ _____. But I_____ interested in computers.

2 A And _____ your husband interested in sport?

B Yes, _____ _____. He's a football fan.

3 A _____ your husband a good cook?

B No, _____ _____.

4 A And you? _____ you a good cook?

B Yes, _____ _____.

5 A _____ your teacher from England?

B No, she_____ _____. She_____ from Canada.

6 A And _____ your business partner Don from Scotland?

B Yes, _____ _____. His family is from Glasgow.

Speaking

Pair work

12 **Ask and answer with a partner.**

Stellen Sie einem anderen Kursmitglied die Fragen aus Übung 10.
Machen Sie sich zu den Antworten Notizen.

(Marianne), are you
a good cook?

No, I'm not.

Yes, I am. And
you, (Marcus)?

Are you interested
in cars?

Whole class

Now answer questions about your partner.

Beantworten Sie Fragen über Ihren Partner / Ihre Partnerin.

CLASS   Is (Marcus/Marianne) a good cook?
YOU   Yes, he/she is. // No, he/she's not.

Pre-task

13 **Please complete.**

Wie lauten die Fragen?

1 *Are you a football fan?* _____ ? – Yes, I am. I'm a big football fan.

2 _____ ? – No, I'm not. I'm not an opera fan.

3 _____ ? – Yes, I am. I'm a coffee drinker.

4 _____ ? – No, I'm not. I'm not a morning person.

5 _____ ? – …

Mini-task

Group work

14 **Find someone who …**

1 *Finden Sie in Ihrer Gruppe:*
   – a tea drinker
   – a football fan
   – a good singer
   – a morning person

2 *Berichten Sie anschließend dem Kurs.*

I can ...

Bewerten Sie Ihren Lernerfolg. Ergänzen Sie.

Folgende Wörter, die ich gelernt habe, sind mir wichtig.

_____

_____

_____

_____

_____

Ich kann:
– *jemandem einen guten Morgen/Abend wünschen.*

   Good _____ / _____ .

– *jemanden fragen, wie es ihm geht.*

   How _____ ?

– *sagen, wie es mir geht.*

   _____ , *thanks.*

– *jemanden nach seiner Telefon- und Handynummer fragen.*

   What _____ , *please?*

   And what _____ , *please?*

– *sagen, wofür ich mich interessiere und nicht interessiere.*

   _I'm_ _____ .

   I'm not _____ .

Außerdem kann ich Folgendes richtig anwenden:

- *die Zahlen 0–10*
- *die Fragewörter who? where? what? und how?*
- *a/an und the*
- *das Plural –s*
- *Are you …? – Yes, I am. / No, I'm not. // Yes, we are. / No, we're not.*
- *Is he/she …? – Yes, he/she is. // No, he's/she's not. // No, he/she isn't.*

My page 3

❶ Greetings

Ergänzen Sie die Dialoge mit Wörtern aus dem Kasten.

evening ● fine ● Good ● How ● morning ● thanks

Dialogue 1:

A Good _____¹. _____²

are you this evening?

B I'm _____³, thanks.

Dialogue 2:

A _____⁴ morning, Renan.

How are you this _____⁵?

C Fine, _____⁶. And you?

❷ Telephone numbers

(20)

Schreiben Sie die Telefonnummern auf, die Sie hören. Hören Sie die Übung anschließend noch einmal und überprüfen Sie Ihre Lösungen.

1 **Christa** _____		4 **Frank** _____	
2 **Doro** _____		5 **Gunther (mobile)** _____	
3 **Isobel (mobile)** _____		6 **Hannah** _____	

❸ Interests & hobbies

Die Geburtstagsgeschenke für Gabi und Tim verraten einiges über ihre Vorlieben. Bilden Sie mit diesen Wörtern Sätze über ihre Hobbys.

- a good cook
- an opera fan
- tennis
- a rock music fan
- horror films
- golf
- the internet

4 More about me

Talking about likes & dislikes • Talking about people & possessions • Numbers 11–100
The simple present (1): statements & questions

Focus 1 *I have / like …*

Reading **1** **Look and read.**

Schauen Sie sich den Cartoon an. Lesen Sie die Texte in den Sprechblasen.

1

You have a big car.

I don't have 'a big car'. I have a 'limo', son.

2

Look. I have a bedroom.

3

And you have a kitchen.

No, this is the bar.

4

I don't have a kitchen – but I have a microwave.

5

Oh, you like pizza.

6

Mama mia, son. I'm Italian.

I don't 'like' pizza. I love pizza!

Now decide.

Welche Sätze könnte der Mann sagen? Markieren Sie die richtigen Sätze (✓).

Yes
- [ ] I have a bar.
- [ ] I have a driver.
- [ ] I have a sauna.
- [ ] I like my car.

No
- [ ] I don't have a bar.
- [ ] I don't have a driver.
- [ ] I don't have a sauna.
- [ ] I don't like my car.

Speaking | **2** | **Please complete.**

Ergänzen Sie die Tabelle mit den Wörtern unten und anderen Wörtern, die Sie kennen.

a daughter

beer • a car • ~~a cat~~
classical music • a daughter
a dog • fast food • fish • football
Formula 1 • a mountain bike
a notebook • a PC • pop music
quiz shows • ~~a son~~ • wine
talk shows

children	*a son,* _____
pets	*a cat,* _____
food	_____
drinks	_____
transport	_____
music	_____
TV programmes	_____
sport	_____
computers	_____

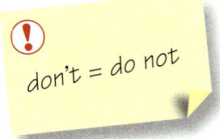

a dog   fish   a notebook

Pair work | **Speak to a partner.**

*Erzählen Sie sich gegenseitig, was Sie haben
bzw. nicht haben und was Sie mögen bzw. nicht mögen.*

> I have two children, two daughters.

> I don't have a pet.

> I like coffee.

> I don't like beer.

> What about you?

Grammar ☞ p. 76

+	–
I / You / We **have** a car.	I / You / We **don't have** a car.
I / You / We **like** pizza.	I / You / We **don't like** pizza.

⚠ *don't = do not*

Writing | **3** | **Please write.**

Schreiben Sie vier Sätze über sich auf einen Zettel – ohne Ihren Namen!

> I have two children.
> I'm not interested in football.
> I love pizza.
> I don't have a pet.

Useful language

(I think) that's (Susanne).
No, it's not me.
(Birgit,) is it you?
Yes, it's me.

Now listen and speak.

Der Kursleiter / Die Kursleiterin liest einige Zettel der Klasse vor. Wer hat sie geschrieben?

Pronunciation **4** (21) **Listen, then listen and repeat.**

[ʃ]	[tʃ]
fish	kitchen
shopping	children
show	match

(22) **Look and listen.**

Pat [paet] is a name.
A pet [pet] is a cat or a dog.

(23) **Now listen, then listen and repeat.**

Pat	fan	sandwich	taxi
hamburger	that	match	thanks

Focus 2 *Do you have / like … ?*

Reading **5** **Read and decide.**

Lesen Sie und entscheiden Sie, wie es nach Bild 3 weitergeht. Nummerieren Sie die restlichen Bilder (4–6).

(24) Now listen and check.

> **Grammar**   ☞ p. 76
>
> | ? | + | – |
> |---|---|---|
> | **Do** you **have** a TV? | Yes, I **do**. | No, I **don't** (= **do not**). |
> | **Do** you **like** TV? | Yes, I **do**. | No, I **don't** (= **do not**). |

Practice **6** **Please complete.**

Ergänzen Sie die Fragen und Antworten mit do *oder* don't *und* have *oder* like.

1 _____ you have a dog? – Yes, I _____. I have a Dobermann.

2 _____ you _____ a bodyguard? – Yes, I _____.

3 _____ two million dollars? – Yes, _____.

4 _____ a billion dollars? – A billion? No, _____.

5 _____ Italian wine? – Yes, _____.

6 _____ you _____ me? – No, _____. You ask too many questions, son.

Pre-task **7** **Ask your teacher.**

Whole class

Stellen Sie Ihrem Kursleiter / Ihrer Kursleiterin Fragen mit Do you have … ? *und*
Do you like … ?

> Do you have children?

> Do you like fish?

> Do you have a pet?

> Do you like swimming?

> Do you have … ?

> Do you like … ?

shopping

cooking

swimming

Pair work **Now ask your partner.**

Mini-task 8

Group work

Make a class profile.

1 *In Gruppen schreiben Sie Fragen mit* Do you have … ? *und* Do you like … ? *auf, die Sie anderen Kursmitgliedern stellen wollen.*

2 *Jedes Gruppenmitglied wählt eine Frage aus und versucht mindestens zwei Kursmitglieder zu finden, die mit* Yes, I do *antworten. Notieren Sie die yes-Antworten.*

3 *Erstellen Sie ein Säulendiagramm und berichten Sie dem Kurs.*

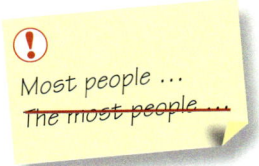
Most people …
~~The most people …~~

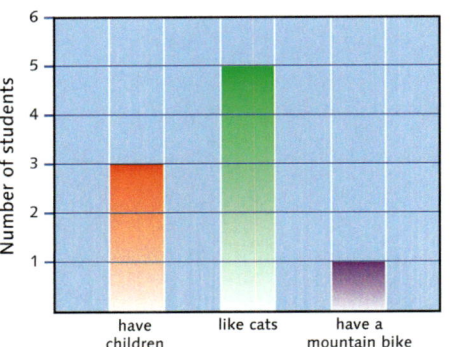

Useful language

(Three) people have / like …
Most people …

Focus 3 *Numbers 11–100*

Speaking 9

Look and speak.

Wie alt schätzen Sie Desmond?

How old is Desmond?

I think he's between
20 (twenty) and 30 (thirty).
30 (thirty) and 40 (forty).
40 (forty) and 50 (fifty).
50 (fifty) and 60 (sixty).
60 (sixty) and 70 (seventy).

How old are you young man? Eight?!

Or eighty-eight?

Now talk about these people.

Useful language

Oh, I don't know.
I think (she's) …
Do you think so?

Serena

Frank

Floyd

Suzy

Vocabulary **10** ## Look and write.

Ergänzen Sie die Tabelle. Schreiben Sie die Zahlen in Worten aus.

1 _____	29 *twenty-nine* _____
2 _____	36 _____
3 _____	43 _____
4 _____	48 _____
5 _____	52 _____
6 _____	66 _____
7 _____	71 _____
8 _____	74 _____
9 _____	88 _____
10 _____	99 _____

11 eleven	17 seventeen	23 twenty-three	29 twenty-nine	70 seventy
12 twelve	18 eighteen	24 twenty-four	30 thirty	80 eighty
13 thirteen	19 nineteen	25 twenty-five	31 thirty-one	90 ninety
14 fourteen	20 twenty	26 twenty-six	40 forty	100 a/one hundred
15 fifteen	21 twenty-one	27 twenty-seven	50 fifty	
16 sixteen	22 twenty-two	28 twenty-eight	60 sixty	

Listening **11** (25) ## Listen and repeat, then listen and decide. Which number is it?

1 ☐ 13 ☐ 30	**6** ☐ 18 ☐ 80
2 ☐ 14 ☐ 40	**7** ☐ 19 ☐ 90
3 ☐ 15 ☐ 50	**8** ☐ 23 ☐ 32
4 ☐ 16 ☐ 60	**9** ☐ 45 ☐ 54
5 ☐ 17 ☐ 70	

Speaking
Pair work
12 ## Say six numbers.

Diktieren Sie Ihrem Partner / Ihrer Partnerin sechs Zahlen zwischen 11 und 40.
Tragen Sie dann die Ihnen diktierten Zahlen auf der Bingokarte unten ein.

Game
Whole class
13 ## Play Bingo.

Wenn eine Zahl ausgerufen wird, die auf Ihrer
Bingokarte steht, streichen Sie sie durch.
Wer zuerst alle Zahlen auf der Karte durchge-
strichen hat, ruft ‚Bingo!' und hat gewonnen.
Sie können Bingo dann noch einmal mit den
Zahlen 41–70 und 71–100 spielen.

I can ...

Bewerten Sie Ihren Lernerfolg. Ergänzen Sie.

Folgende Wörter, die ich gelernt habe, sind mir wichtig.

_____

_____

_____

_____

_____

Ich kann:
– *sagen, ob ich Kinder habe oder nicht.*

   I _____ .

– *sagen, was ich habe und nicht habe.*

   I have _____ .

   I don't _____ .

– *sagen, was ich mag und nicht mag.*

   I like _____ .

   I _____ .

– *jemandem entsprechende Fragen stellen.*

   Do you have children / a cat / ... _____ ?

   Do you like shopping / fish / ... _____ ?

– *sagen, wie alt jemand ist.*

   He's ... / between ... and .... _____ .

Außerdem kann ich Folgendes richtig anwenden:

• *Sätze mit I/you/we + Verb bzw. mit don't*
• *Fragen mit do*
• *Die Zahlen 11–100*

My page 4

❶ Things we have & like

a Finden Sie im Rätsel zwölf Wörter.

b Tragen Sie die Lösungen aus Übung 1a in die richtige Kategorie ein.

food	drinks	pets

children	music	sport

f	o	o	t	b	a	l	l	r	t
s	j	r	r	d	b	o	e	c	c
x	y	o	e	t	p	t	k	o	a
d	o	g	g	e	h	u	v	f	t
p	o	p	r	g	b	f	x	f	o
d	p	a	u	s	i	x	r	e	g
a	s	a	b	g	o	n	r	e	n
z	d	h	m	c	m	n	g	k	h
o	z	p	a	z	z	i	p	w	l
u	z	o	h	m	w	n	s	u	v

❷ Do you have … ? / Do you like … ?

Formulieren Sie die passenden Fragen zu diesen Antworten.

1 *Do you like Italian food?*
Italian food? Yes, I do.

2 _____ ?
Oh, yes, I like red wine.

3 _____ ?
No, I don't, but I have a cat.

4 _____ ?
Sport? No, I don't.

5 _____ ?
Yes, I do. I like computers.

6 _____ ?
A car? No, I don't.

❸ I have … / I like …

26 a Hören Sie dem Gespräch über Familie und Interessen zwischen Jim und May zu. Wer hat welche Vorlieben?

	Jim	May		Jim	May
TV			pop music		
radio			DVD player		
classical			children		
CD player					

b Hören Sie noch einmal zu und machen Sie einen Kreis um die Zahlen, die im Gespräch vorkommen.

TV channels* 16/36/60   DVDs 19/90/99
CDs 15/25/50   children 3/13/30

*Kanäle

Quick Check 1

1 Vocabulary

8 points

Your score

8

Finden Sie für die Satzanfänge (1–8) die passenden Fortsetzungen (a–h).

1 Nice	a two sons.
2 How	b are you from?
3 What's	c Poland.
4 Where	d married?
5 What's your	e name?
6 I have	f your phone number?
7 I'm from	g to meet you.
8 Are you	h are you?

2 am/is/are

10 points

Your score

10

Kreuzen Sie die richtige Verbform an.

1 I ☐ am ☐ is a good swimmer.

2 Thomas and Joe ☐ is ☐ are taxi drivers.

3 How ☐ are ☐ is you today, Peter?

4 My sister's name ☐ are ☐ is Susan.

5 ☐ Are ☐ Is her husband's name John?

6 Julie's brothers ☐ aren't ☐ isn't interested in football.

7 I ☐ am ☐ is married. Jane ☐ are ☐ is married too.

8 Harry and Peg ☐ aren't ☐ isn't from New York. They ☐ are ☐ is from New Jersey.

3 Pronouns

12 points

Your score

12

Vervollständigen Sie die Dialoge mit Wörtern aus dem Kasten.

he ● he ● her ● his ● it ● my ● my ● she ● she ● you ● ~~your~~ ● your ● your

Dialogue 1:

A What's *your*[1] surname, please?

B _____'s[2] Alton.

A And _____[3] first name?

B Diana.

A Is this _____[4] daughter?

B Yes. _____[5] name is Mary. _____'s[6] three.

Dialogue 2:

C This is _____[1] son. _____[2] name is Peter.

D Oh. How old is _____[3]?

C _____'s[4] ten.

D _____[5] daughter's name is Petra. _____'s[6] ten too.

C Oh. Nice to meet _____[7], Petra.

4 *How ... ? What ... ?*
Where ... ?
Who ... ?

8 points

Your score

8

Ergänzen Sie die Fragen mit den richtigen Fragewörtern.

1 _____ are you? – Fine, thanks.

2 _____ is an opera fan? – Molly.

3 _____ are you from? – Italy.

4 _____'s your mobile number? – It's 0171087545.

5 _____ is from Russia? – Dmitri.

6 _____'s your favourite food? – Pizza.

7 _____'s Sally? – She's in London.

8 _____ do you say this word? – Sorry, I don't know.

5 **Reading & listening** ⑳27

8 points

Your score

8

a *Lesen Sie die Anzeigen. Welcher Text ist von Paula und welcher von Ken?* *(Kreisen)* *Sie in jedem Bild vier Entscheidungskriterien ein.*

He – 49
I like good food and good wine. I'm a pop music fan. I have a big car and a big house with a sauna. I'm not interested in cats and dogs. No children, please. Call me! ☎ 0121

He – 32
Do you like sport? Do you like children and pets? Do you like good music? I like jogging and fitness. I have two children and a dog. I'm interested in pop music. ☎ 0123

She – 34
I like children, pets and good food. I'm not interested in sport. ☎ 0125

He – 29
Do you like opera? Do you like good food and wine? Do you like cats? Then I like you. Please phone me. ☎ 0122

She – 30
Where are you? Do you like red wine, Italian food, good music and cats? ☎ 0126

She – 29
Where is my partner? Do you like good food? Are you interested in sport? I like children and pets. ☎ 0124

Your score

2

Total score

48

b *Lesen Sie die Anzeigen noch einmal und finden Sie geeignete Partner für Paula und Ken.*

c *Hören Sie nun zu und überprüfen Sie Ihre Antworten.*

5 Families

Talking about families • Talking about jobs & places • *they're – their*
The simple present (2)

Focus 1 *Relations*

Speaking 1 Look and speak.

Wer sind diese Prominenten und wie sind sie miteinander verwandt?

Useful language

They're …

… is …'s   mother.
          father.
          daughter.
          son.
          sister.
          brother.
          wife.
          husband.

Charlie & Geraldine ● Elizabeth & Charles
Kirk & Michael ● Bill & Hillary ● Marge & Bart
Michael & Ralf ● Serena & Venus

Elizabeth's son
~~the son of Elizabeth~~

They're Charlie and Geraldine Chaplin.

They're father and daughter.

Geraldine is Charlie's daughter.

Practice | **2** | # Read and decide.

Schauen Sie sich Sätze 1–2 genau an. Wählen Sie danach
bei den Sätzen 3–8 zwischen they're und their.

1 **They're** father and daughter.

2 **Their** surname is Chaplin.

3 ☐ They're / ☐ Their Formula 1 drivers.

4 ☐ They're / ☐ Their surname is Williams.

5 ☐ They're / ☐ Their daughter's name is Chelsea.

6 ☐ They're / ☐ Their mother and son.

7 ☐ They're / ☐ Their best films are *Spartacus* and *Basic Instinct*.

8 ☐ They're / ☐ Their cartoon characters.

⚠️ they're … = they are …
sie sind …
their surname = ihr Familienname

Pre-task | **3** | # Look and speak.

Whole class

Wer ist wer? Verwenden Sie die Wörter aus Übung 1.

Lisa is Marge's daughter.

Mini-task | **4** | # Ask and answer.

Pair work

1 Schreiben Sie die Namen einiger Ihrer Familienmitglieder auf einen Zettel.

2 Zeigen Sie den Zettel Ihrem Partner / Ihrer Partnerin, beantworten Sie seine/ihre Fragen. Achtung: Heben Sie den Zettel auf, Sie werden ihn noch einmal benötigen!

Useful language

Who is … ?
Sorry, how do you say this name?
He's my father/brother/son/husband/partner.
She's my mother/sister/daughter/wife/partner.
Is … your (partner)? – Yes, he/she is. // No, he/she isn't.
How old is … ?
He's/She's (sixteen/sixty).

Focus 2 *How people live*

Reading **5** **Read and answer.**

1 Who are ex-husband and ex-wife?

2 Who are brother and sister?

3 Who is Suzy's father?

First name	Serena	Frank	Floyd	Suzy
Surname	Miller	Miller	Harvey	Miller
Married?	Divorced, one daughter	Remarried, two daughters	Married, no children	Single, no children
Parents	Primrose & Denzel Harvey	Margaret & Bill Miller	Primrose & Denzel Harvey	Serena & Frank Miller
From	Newark, USA	Hull, England	Newark, USA	London
Home now	London	Hull, England	Boston, USA	London
Job	Café owner	Retired	Teacher	Clown

Now read and decide.

Markieren Sie die Informationen im Text, die in der Tabelle oben nicht enthalten sind.

Serena Miller is divorced and lives in west London. She has a daughter, Suzy, but Suzy doesn't live with her mother. Suzy lives in north London. Serena has a café in the centre of London. The name of the café is *First Choice*. Serena works hard, and she likes her job. But she doesn't have much free time.

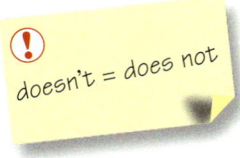

doesn't = does not

Grammar
☞ p. 76

He/She/It		**lives**	in west London.	[live + **s**]
He/She/It	**doesn't**	**live**	in the centre of London.	[do**es**n't + live]
He/She/It		live**s**/work**s**/like**s**/ha**s**/…		
He/She/It	**doesn't**	live/work/like/have/…		

| Practice | **6** | **Read and decide. (✓)** |

Sind die Aussagen wahr (true) *oder falsch* (false)?

True False

1 ☐ ☐ Serena comes from the USA.

2 ☐ ☐ She lives in north London.

3 ☐ ☐ Frank doesn't live with Serena or Suzy.

4 ☐ ☐ He doesn't have a job.

5 ☐ ☐ Floyd lives in the USA.

6 ☐ ☐ He works in a school.

7 ☐ ☐ Suzy doesn't live in London.

8 ☐ ☐ She has an office job.

Now speak.

Korrigieren Sie die falschen Aussagen. Sagen Sie, was stimmt.

| Practice | **7** | **What is right? (✓)** |

1 Does Floyd have children? ☐ Yes, he does. ☐ No, he doesn't.

2 Does he have a sister? ☐ Yes, he does. ☐ No, he doesn't.

3 Does he live in Boston? ☐ Yes, he does. ☐ No, he doesn't.

4 Does Frank live in London? ☐ Yes, he does. ☐ No, he doesn't.

5 Does he have a son? ☐ Yes, he does. ☐ No, he doesn't.

6 Does Serena have a good job? ☐ Yes, she does. ☐ No, she doesn't.

7 Does she have a son? ☐ Yes, she does. ☐ No, she doesn't.

8 Does Suzy have children? ☐ Yes, she does. ☐ No, she doesn't.

Grammar   ☞ p. 76

Does he/she/it work?   Yes, he/she/it **does**.
                            No, he/she/it **doesn't**.

| Pre-task | **8** | **Complete the questions and answers.** |

1 <u>Does</u> Serena <u>work</u> in an office? – No, she _____.

2 _____ she work in the centre of London? – Yes, she _____.

3 _____ she _____ there too? – No, she _____. She lives in west London.

4 _____ she _____ alone? – Yes, she _____. But she has a cat.

5 _____ she _____ a car? – No, she _____. But she can drive.

6 _____ she _____ London? – Yes, she _____. She thinks it's a great place.

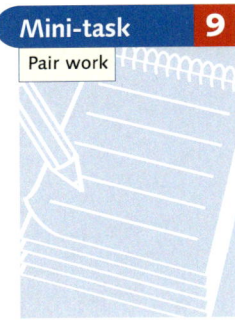

Mini-task **9**

Pair work

Find out more about the people in exercise 4.

Lassen Sie sich noch einmal den Zettel mit den Namen aus Übung 4 zeigen. Stellen Sie Fragen, um mehr über die Personen herauszufinden.

Useful language

Does (Anita)	*live here in (Leipzig)?*	*— Yes, (she) does. /*
		No, (she) doesn't. (She lives in Dessau.)
Does (she)	*like it here / there?*	*Is (she) married?* *— Yes, (she) is.*
	have a family?	*— No, (she) isn't.*
	have children?	
	have a job / a good job?	
	have a car?	
	have a pet?	

Now report to the class.

Helga has a sister.
Her name is Anita.
She lives in Dessau.
She is married and has
two children.

Pronunciation **10**

(28) **Listen and repeat.**

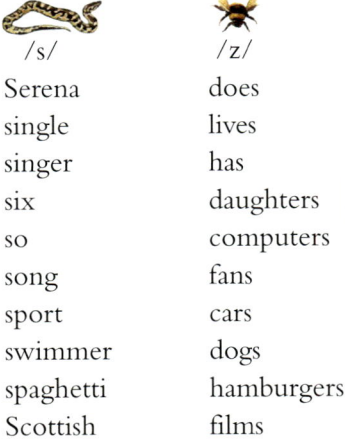

/s/	/z/
Serena	does
single	lives
singer	has
six	daughters
so	computers
song	fans
sport	cars
swimmer	dogs
spaghetti	hamburgers
Scottish	films

Serena lives in London.
Suzy lives in London too.
Suzy is single, she has no daughters.
Sport is so good for you.
Do Scottish swimmers like spaghetti?

Focus 3 *Partners & families*

Reading **11** ## Read and decide.

Lesen Sie die Texte, ergänzen Sie die Tabelle und entscheiden Sie, wer mit wem als Paar zusammenlebt.

	from?	married?	children?	pets?	good food / cook?	computer?	car?
Sam							
Pedro							
Jenny							
Fiona							

This is Sam. He's from London. Sam is married and has two daughters, Emma and Caroline. Sam's  family has pets – four cats! Sam likes eBay, and is a good cook. The family has a car, but Sam doesn't drive.

Sam

This is Pedro. He's from the USA, but he lives in Europe now, in London. Pedro is not married, but he and his partner  have two sons, Mike and Johnny. Pedro likes the internet and has a computer in the bedroom – his partner doesn't like that! Pedro and his partner don't have a car.

Pedro

This is Jenny. Her family is from Hong Kong, but she lives in London now. Jenny is a computer expert. Her partner is interested  in computers too. They have one at home. Jenny and her partner have two children, but they don't have a pet.

Jenny

This is Fiona Thomas. Her family is from Canada, but she lives in London now with her partner and children. Fiona likes computers, cats and cars. She drives a  German Golf, but her partner doesn't drive. She likes good food too. Her partner's family is from London. Well, he's not just her 'partner', he's her husband.

Fiona

Now decide.

Lesen Sie die Sätze. Welche Person(en) aus den Texten oben ist/sind jeweils gemeint?

1 They have a computer in the bedroom.
2 His wife likes cars.
3 They have two daughters.
4 She doesn't drive a Golf.
5 They don't have a car.
6 They don't have a cat.
7 She comes from North America.
8 His partner comes from Asia.

Listening **12** (29) **Listen and decide.**

Hören Sie ein Gespräch und entscheiden Sie, welche Personen aus Übung 11 gemeint sind. Wer genau ist das Kind? Wie heißen seine Mutter und sein Vater?

I can ...

Bewerten Sie Ihren Lernerfolg. Ergänzen Sie.

Folgende Wörter, die ich gelernt habe, sind mir wichtig.

_____

_____

_____

_____

_____

Ich kann:
– *über meine Familienangehörigen sprechen und sagen, wie sie heißen und*
  wie alt sie sind.

_____*is my*_____ . *He's/She's* _____ .

_____*is/are my*_____ . *He's/She's/They're* _____ .

– *sagen, wo meine Familienangehörigen leben und arbeiten.*

   He _____ .

   She _____ .

   They _____ .

– *jemandem entsprechende Fragen stellen.*

   Does your brother/... _____ ?

   Do your parents/... _____ ?

Außerdem kann ich Folgendes richtig anwenden:

• *Sätze mit he/she/it + Verb mit -s bzw. mit doesn't*
• *Fragen mit does*

My page 5

Culture link 🔗

In den englischsprachigen Ländern wird nicht so deutlich differenziert zwischen ‚Freund' und ‚Bekannter': das Wort *friend* kann auch jemanden beschreiben, den man nicht sehr gut kennt.

1 **Families**

a *Suchen Sie im Rätsel acht Familienwörter.*

Across
4
7
8

Down
1
2
3
5
6

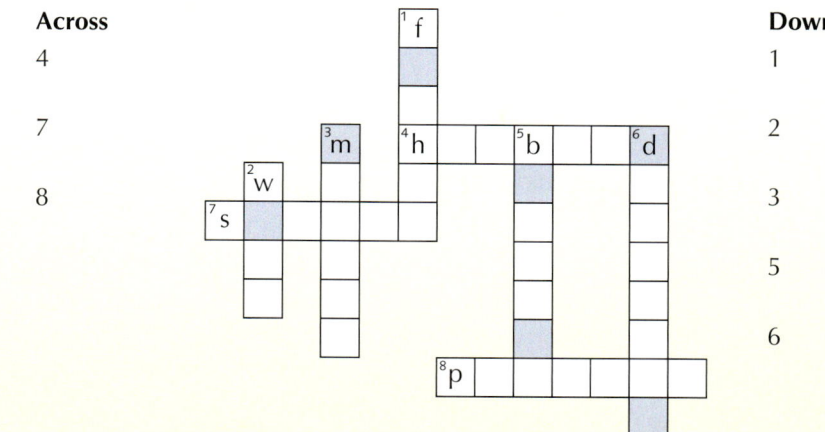

b *Benutzen Sie die Buchstaben in den blauen Quadraten, um ein weiteres Familienwort zu bilden.*

30 **2** **Who's who?**

Hören Sie zu und kreuzen Sie das passende Satzende an.

So lernen Sie am besten Wortschatz 1

Beim Wortschatzlernen gilt zunächst das, was bereits im Lerntipp von Unit 2 gesagt wurde: lieber wenig und oft. Nehmen Sie sich nie mehr als 8 bis 10 neue Vokabeln auf einmal vor. Achten Sie darauf, die Wörter immer als Teil einer Redewendung oder eines Satzes zu lernen. Denn sicher haben Sie schon gemerkt, dass es oft keine eins zu eins-Entsprechungen gibt.

1 Ken is Sarah's
2 Toby and Lucy are
3 Valerie is Lucy's
4 Marion is Sarah's
5 Fiona and Lauren are
6 Anna is Ken's

☐ partner
☐ brother and sister
☐ sister
☐ mother
☐ mother and daughter
☐ wife

☐ husband.
☐ husband and wife.
☐ daughter.
☐ sister.
☐ sisters.
☐ daughter.

3 **have / like / live / work**
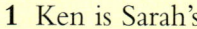

Streichen Sie die falschen Verbformen durch.

1 Betty work / works in a café.
2 I like / likes pizza.
3 They live / lives in London.
4 He have / has a car.

5 I don't like / doesn't like beer.
6 She don't live / doesn't live in Paris.
7 We have / has one daughter.
8 You don't work / doesn't work in London.

6 *My week*

Telling the time • Talking about TV schedules • Times of the day • Days of the week

Focus 1 *The time*

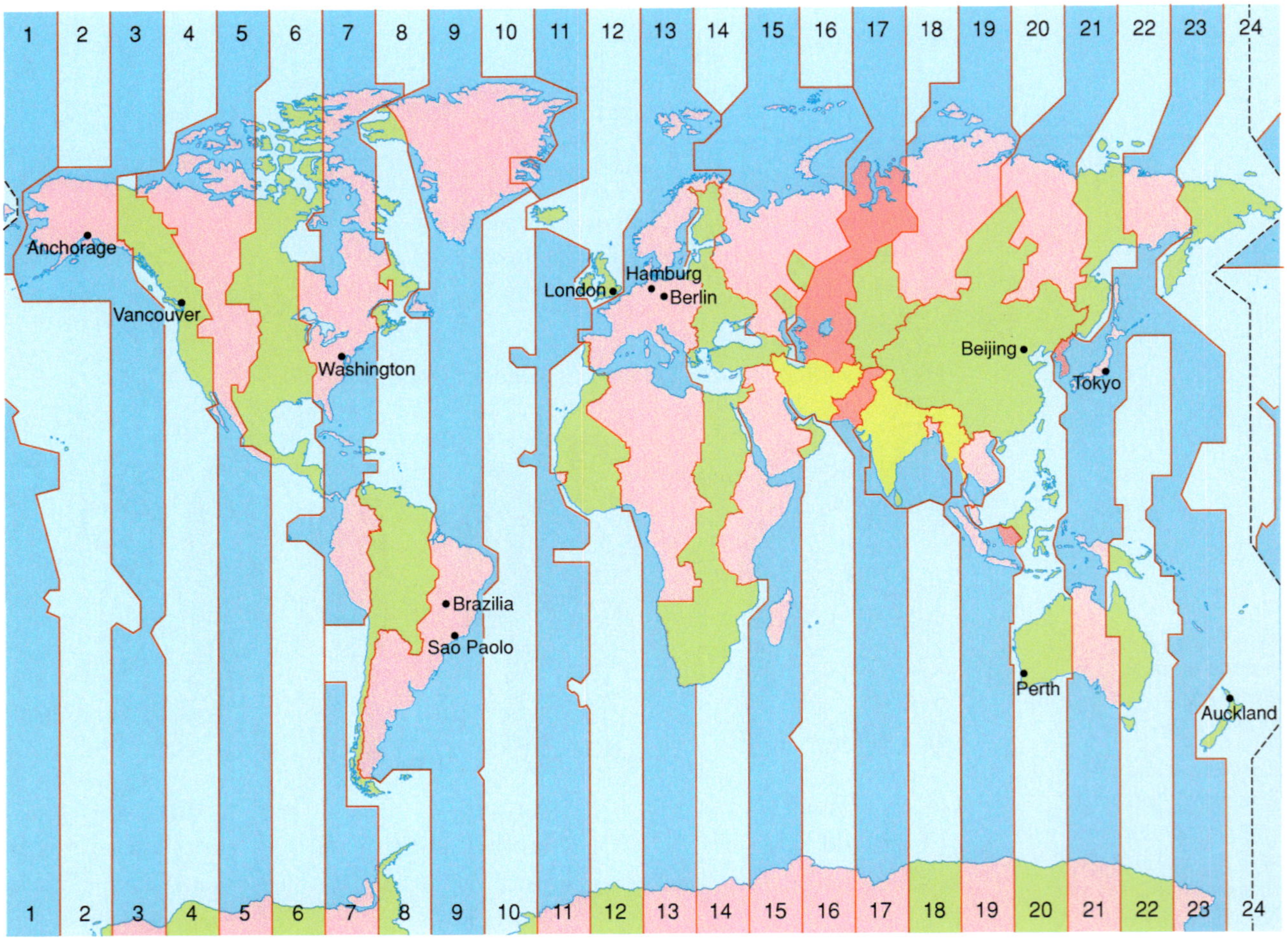

| 1 | 2 | 3 | 4 | 5 | 6 | 7 | 8 | 9 | 10 | 11 | 12 | 13 | 14 | 15 | 16 | 17 | 18 | 19 | 20 | 21 | 22 | 23 | 24 |

Anchorage
Vancouver
Washington
London• Hamburg •Berlin
Beijing• •Tokyo
•Brazilia
Sao Paolo
Perth
Auckland

| 1 | 2 | 3 | 4 | 5 | 6 | 7 | 8 | 9 | 10 | 11 | 12 | 13 | 14 | 15 | 16 | 17 | 18 | 19 | 20 | 21 | 22 | 23 | 24 |

Marina

Bruno

Amy

Alice and Patrick

Dominic

Speaking
Whole class

1 **Look and match.**

Schauen Sie sich die Weltzeitkarte an. Ordnen Sie die Uhrzeiten den Orten zu.

1 four o'clock in the morning
2 seven o'clock in the morning
3 twelve o'clock in the morning
4 eight o'clock in the evening
5 twelve o'clock at night

a Auckland (New Zealand)
b London (UK)
c Perth (Australia)
d Vancouver (Canada)
e Washington (USA)

Look and speak.

Nun schauen Sie sich die Fotos an. Wo befinden sich die Personen gerade?

> at home in the kitchen • at home on the sofa
> at work • in bed asleep • in bed with a book

Useful language

*(Amy) is (in bed with a book).
So it must be (evening or night).
Or it's (morning).
I think it's (evening or night).
Then (Amy) must be in (Auckland) because (in Auckland it's twelve o'clock at night).*

Look and decide.

Und nun schlussfolgern Sie aus dem, was Sie sehen können, in welcher Stadt sich die Personen aufhalten.

Practice
Pair work

2 **Ask and answer.**

Schauen Sie sich die Weltzeitkarte an. Stellen Sie und beantworten Sie die Fragen.

When it's twelve o'clock in the morning in Britain (London), what time is it in ...

1 Germany (Hamburg)?
2 China (Beijing)?
3 Japan (Tokyo)?
4 Alaska (Anchorage)?
5 Brazil (Sao Paolo, Brasilia)?

What time is it?
Nine o'clock.

What?!

It's nine o'clock – in Moscow.

In Moscow?
07:00 A.M. APRIL 1
Yes, it's nine o'clock in Moscow and it's seven o'clock here. April Fool!

Vocabulary **3** **Look and complete.**

Welche Uhren zeigen die folgenden Zeiten an? Ergänzen Sie.

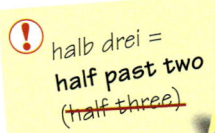
halb drei = **half past two** (half three)

- five to three
- three o'clock
- twenty past two
- ten to three
- twenty-five past two
- twenty to three

1  It's two o'clock.

2 It's five past two.

3  It's ten past two.

4  It's quarter past two.

5  It's _____ .

6  It's _____ .

7  It's half past two.

8  It's twenty-five to three.

9  It's _____ .

10  It's quarter to three.

TO   PAST

11  It's _____ .

12  It's _____ .

13  It's _____ .

Pair work **Now ask and answer.**

A What time is it on clock number (five)?

B It's (twenty past two).

Listening **4** **Listen and match.**

Sie hören drei Kurzdialoge und zwei Ansagen (am Flughafen). Ordnen Sie die richtigen Uhrzeiten zu.

a  □
b  □
c  □
d  □
e  □

Practice **5** **Ask and answer.**

Pair work

Zeichnen Sie 8 Uhren. Auf 1–4 zeichnen Sie vier verschiedene Uhrzeiten. Schreiben Sie die Uhrzeiten unter jede Uhr. Danach fragen Sie Ihren Partner / Ihre Partnerin nach seinen/ihren Uhrzeiten. Zeichnen Sie die Uhrzeiten auf den Uhren 5–8.

Useful language

OK, number one.

What time is it, please?

It's …

Thanks.

Focus 2 *The days of the week*

Vocabulary **6** (32) **Listen and repeat.**

5 Monday **6 Tuesday** **7 Wednesday** **8 Thursday** **9 Friday** **10 Saturday** **11 Sunday**

Now ask and answer.

Which day comes before (Thursday)?
Which day comes after (Monday)?
Which day comes between (Monday) and (Wednesday)?

Pre-task **7** **Read and complete.**

Lesen Sie das Fernsehprogramm und ergänzen Sie die Sätze 1–4 unten mit den Namen der Sendungen.

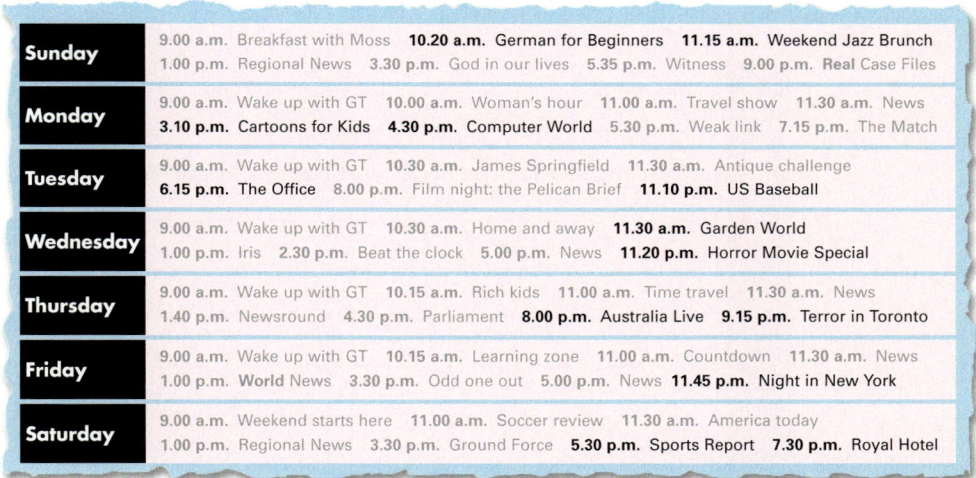

Sunday	9.00 a.m. Breakfast with Moss 10.20 a.m. German for Beginners 11.15 a.m. Weekend Jazz Brunch 1.00 p.m. Regional News 3.30 p.m. God in our lives 5.35 p.m. Witness 9.00 p.m. Real Case Files
Monday	9.00 a.m. Wake up with GT 10.00 a.m. Woman's hour 11.00 a.m. Travel show 11.30 a.m. News 3.10 p.m. Cartoons for Kids 4.30 p.m. Computer World 5.30 p.m. Weak link 7.15 p.m. The Match
Tuesday	9.00 a.m. Wake up with GT 10.30 a.m. James Springfield 11.30 a.m. Antique challenge 6.15 p.m. The Office 8.00 p.m. Film night: the Pelican Brief 11.10 p.m. US Baseball
Wednesday	9.00 a.m. Wake up with GT 10.30 a.m. Home and away 11.30 a.m. Garden World 1.00 p.m. Iris 2.30 p.m. Beat the clock 5.00 p.m. News 11.20 p.m. Horror Movie Special
Thursday	9.00 a.m. Wake up with GT 10.15 a.m. Rich kids 11.00 a.m. Time travel 11.30 a.m. News 1.40 p.m. Newsround 4.30 p.m. Parliament 8.00 p.m. Australia Live 9.15 p.m. Terror in Toronto
Friday	9.00 a.m. Wake up with GT 10.15 a.m. Learning zone 11.00 a.m. Countdown 11.30 a.m. News 1.00 p.m. World News 3.30 p.m. Odd one out 5.00 p.m. News 11.45 p.m. Night in New York
Saturday	9.00 a.m. Weekend starts here 11.00 a.m. Soccer review 11.30 a.m. America today 1.00 p.m. Regional News 3.30 p.m. Ground Force 5.30 p.m. Sports Report 7.30 p.m. Royal Hotel

1 _____ is on Wednesday at twenty past eleven in the evening.

2 _____ is on Monday at half past four in the afternoon.

3 _____ is on Saturday at half past five in the afternoon.

4 _____ is on Thursday at quarter past nine in the evening.

Now ask and answer questions. Example:

1 What day is Royal Hotel? And what time is it?

2 When is Garden World?

on Thursday
at eight o'clock
in the evening

Mini-task | **8**
Group work

Write a quiz.

Schreiben Sie ein Quiz über Fernsehsendungen hier bei uns.

1 *Machen Sie eine Liste von Sendungen, die Sie kennen oder gern sehen.*

2 *Arbeiten Sie in Gruppen. Wählen Sie fünf Sendungen aus und notieren Sie nun fünf Fragen wie diese:*

> When is Lindenstraße?
> A On Saturday at 17.15.
> B On Sunday at 18.40.
> C On Tuesday at 19.30.

Useful language

When is (PlusMinus)?
I don't know (I don't watch it).
Do you watch (PlusMinus)?
– Yes, I do. (I think) It's on … at …
So (B) is the right answer.

> ! Lindenstraße is a programme.
> ARD is a channel (programme).

3 *Tauschen Sie Ihr Quiz mit dem einer anderen Gruppe.*

4 *Lösen Sie deren Quiz und überprüfen Sie Ihre Antworten.*

Song | **9**

(33) **Listen and decide.**

Hören Sie sich das Lied an. Welche Wochentage kommen darin vor?

Group work *Welche Lieder kennen Sie, in denen einer oder mehrere der Tage vorkommen?*

I can …

Bewerten Sie Ihren Lernerfolg. Ergänzen Sie.

Folgende Wörter, die ich gelernt habe, sind mir wichtig.

_____

_____

_____

_____

_____

Ich kann:
– nach der Uhrzeit fragen und Fragen danach beantworten.
  What _____ , *please?*
  Sorry, I don't know. / It's seven o' _____ . / *It's five* _____ / *to eight.*
– fragen, wann etwas im Fernsehen läuft und darauf antworten.
  _____ 'PlusMinus'?
  'It's _____ Monday _____ half past seven _____ the evening.

Außerdem kann ich Folgendes richtig anwenden:

• *die Uhrzeit*

• *die Wochentage*

• *Ausdrücke der Zeit wie* on Sunday, in the morning, at 6 o'clock

My page 6

❶ Days of the week

Ergänzen Sie den Kalender.

1	Monday
2	
3	
4	
5	
6	
7	

❷ Hobbies

34 *Hören Sie zu. An welchen Tagen gehen die Sprecher welchen Hobbys nach?*

1	go swimming		**a**	Monday, Tuesday and Wednesday
2	go to an English class		**b**	Monday, Wednesday and Thursday
3	play tennis at the sports club		**c**	Tuesday and Friday
4	do bodybuilding and gymnastics		**d**	Thursday and Friday
5	go to the disco		**e**	Saturday, Sunday or Tuesday
6	learn jazz dance		**f**	Saturday, Sunday and Thursday

❸ What time is it?

35

a *Hören Sie zu und machen Sie einen Kreis um die Uhrzeiten, die genannt werden.*

| 09:30 | 10:30 | 11:30 | 12:30 | 13:45 | 14:15 | 19:45 | 20:15 |

b *Hören Sie jetzt noch einmal zu und schreiben Sie die Uhrzeiten auf.*

1 It's _____

2 _____

3 _____

4 _____

❹ On Monday, at 10 o'clock in the morning …

Ergänzen Sie mit in, on *oder* at.

Monday? I have a lot to do _____ [1] Monday. I have the doctor _____ [2] 9 o'clock _____ [3] the morning and my English class starts _____ [4] 10.30. My mother and I go for lunch every Monday _____ [5] one o'clock. I always go jogging with Patsy _____ [6] the afternoon, then Jim gets home from work _____ [7] five. I can meet you _____ [8] the evening.

7 *A day in my life*

Talking about daily routines • The simple present with time adverbials

Focus 1 *My routine*

eat in the evening

get up

have lunch

go to bed

Speaking **1** ### Ask and answer.

Pair work

Um wieviel Uhr tun Sie diese Dinge? Sprechen Sie mit einem Partner / einer Partnerin.

1 When do you get up in the week?

2 Do you get up later at the weekend?

3 When do you have lunch on a weekday?

4 And when do you eat in the evening?

5 When do you go to bed on Friday and Saturday?

6 What about Sunday? When do you go to bed then?

When do you get up in the week?

At half past six. And you?

I get up at six o'clock.

Do you get up later at the weekend?

Yes, at eight or nine o'clock. And you?

Remember

on Monday, **on** a weekday
at eight o'clock, **at** the weekend
in the evening, **in** the week

Pronunciation 2

36 Listen and repeat.

When do you get up?

Do you eat breakfast?

When do you start work?

I have breakfast at seven o'clock.

Do you have a coffee break in the morning?

I get up later at the weekend.

Vocabulary 3

Pair work

Look and complete.

Ergänzen Sie die Tabelle mit Ausdrücken aus dem Kasten. Drei Ausdrücke sind bereits eingetragen.

cook/eat in the evening • finish work and go home • ~~go to bed and read/sleep~~ • have a coffee break • ~~have breakfast~~ • ~~have lunch~~ • wake up and get up • start work • leave home and go to work

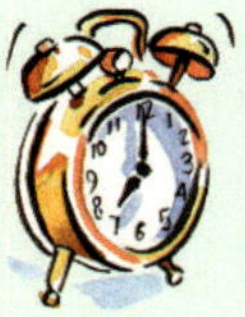	______________	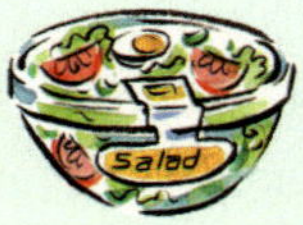	*have lunch*
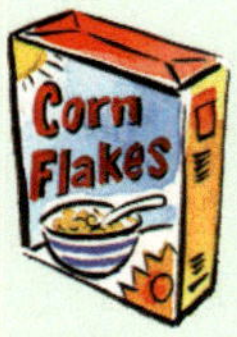	*have breakfast*	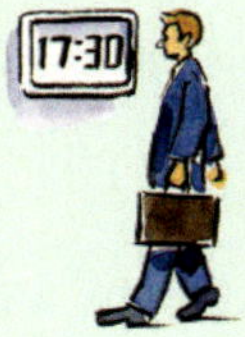	______________
	______________	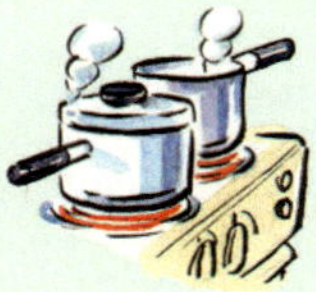	______________
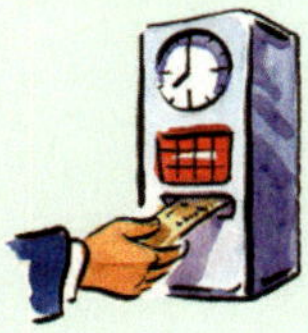	______________	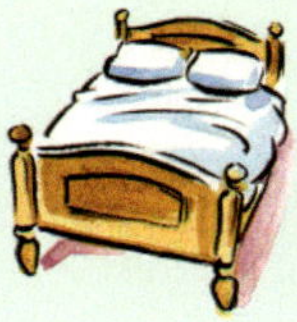	*go to bed and read/sleep*
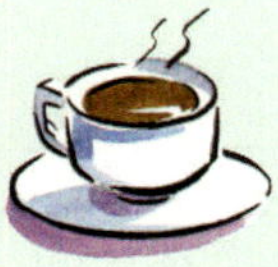	______________		

Reading

Pair work

4 **Read and guess.**

Schauen Sie sich die Fotos an. Lesen Sie danach die Sätze und raten Sie, wer von den beiden Personen jeweils gemeint ist. Schreiben Sie entweder K oder C in die Kästchen.

Kim is a waitress. She works in a bistro.

Christine is a systems administrator. She works on the morning shift in a big factory.

(!)

Kim is **a** waitress.
~~Kim is waitress.~~

1 She starts work at half past eleven in the morning. ☐
2 She starts work at six o'clock in the morning. ☐
3 She finishes work at eleven in the evening. ☐
4 She works at the weekend. ☐
5 She gets up at half past four. ☐
6 She goes home at two o'clock in the afternoon. ☐
7 She goes jogging in the afternoon. ☐
8 She goes to bed at ten o'clock. ☐
9 She goes out with her dog in the afternoon. ☐
10 She has a coffee break (and breakfast) at nine o'clock. ☐

(37) **Now listen and check.**

Speaking

5 **Look and speak.**

Wie unterscheidet sich Ihr Tagesablauf von Kims/Christines?

Kim Christine	gets up starts work has breakfast has a coffee break finishes work goes home goes to bed	at …	And I But I (don't)	get up start work have breakfast have a coffee break finish work go home go to bed	at …	(too).

Christine starts work at six o'clock, but I start at eight.

She gets up at half past four, but I don't get up at half past four!

Focus 2 *always, usually, often, …*

6

Read and decide.

Lesen Sie die Sätze. Bringen Sie dann die Bilder in die richtige Reihenfolge (1–5), passend zu den Sätzen.

1 He usually gets up late.

2 He doesn't have breakfast. He never has time.

3 He often gets to work late.

4 He always sleeps on the train home.

5 He sometimes misses his stop.

always   usually   often   sometimes   never

7

Please complete.

Benutzen Sie always, sometimes … *um zutreffende Aussagen über sich zu machen.*

Example:

I *sometimes* get to work late.

I _____ get up late on Sunday.

I _____ listen to classical music in the evening.

I _____ work at the weekend.

I _____ drink coffee for breakfast.

I _____ sing in the bath.

Grammar   ☞ p. 76

I		**always**	get up	early.
We		**usually**	eat	in the evening.
They		**often**	eat	at a pizzeria.
Tom		**sometimes**	has	lunch in the canteen.
We		**never**	go	to a restaurant.

| I | don't | **always** | eat | lunch. |
| He | doesn't | **often** | eat | breakfast. |

| We | | **often** | watch | TV | in the week / on Saturday / in the evening. |

Practice   **8**   **Make sentences.**

Bringen Sie die Satzteile in die richtige Reihenfolge.

1 always / I / at 6.00 in the week / get up

2 We / go to bed / usually / at 11.00 or 11.30 at the weekend

3 in the morning / They / work / never

4 don't / in the evening / You / often / cook

5 don't / We / have breakfast / often / on Saturday

6 eats / sometimes / lunch in the canteen / Jenny

Pre-task   **9**   **Please match.**

Pair work

Ordnen Sie die Fragen den Antworten auf Seite 57 zu.

  1 When do you get up? □

  2 Do you eat breakfast? *e*

  3 When do you have breakfast? □

  4 When do you start work? □

  5 Do you have a coffee break in the morning? □

  6 When do you have lunch? □

  7 When do you eat in the evening? □

  8 Do you cook in the evening? □

  9 What do you do in the evening? □

10 When do you usually go to bed? □

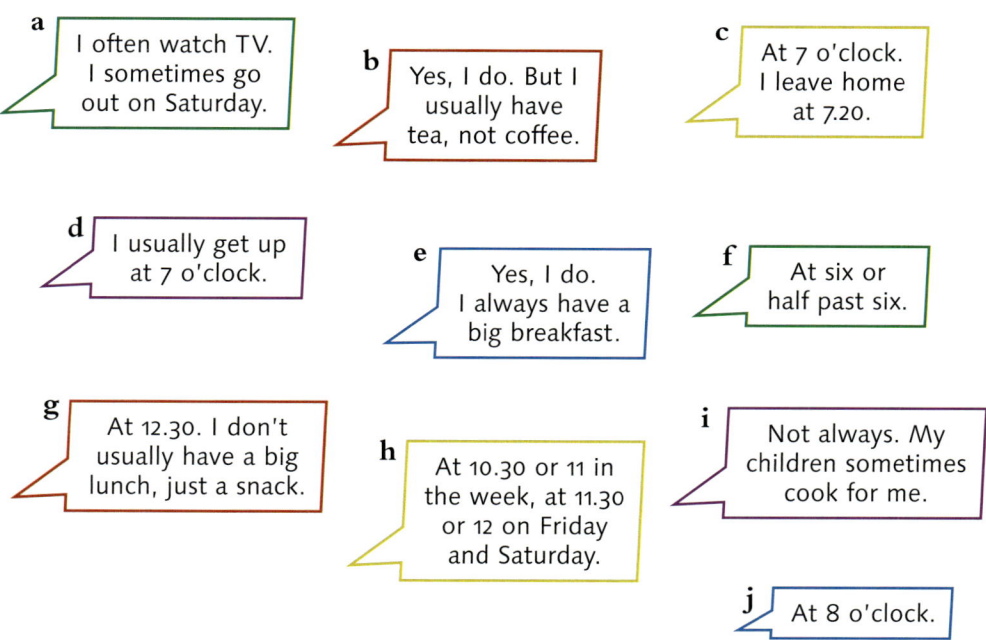

a I often watch TV. I sometimes go out on Saturday.

b Yes, I do. But I usually have tea, not coffee.

c At 7 o'clock. I leave home at 7.20.

d I usually get up at 7 o'clock.

e Yes, I do. I always have a big breakfast.

f At six or half past six.

g At 12.30. I don't usually have a big lunch, just a snack.

h At 10.30 or 11 in the week, at 11.30 or 12 on Friday and Saturday.

i Not always. My children sometimes cook for me.

j At 8 o'clock.

Mini-task 10 **Pair work**

Make a timeline.

1 Arbeiten Sie mit einem neuen Partner / einer neuen Partnerin zusammen. Stellen Sie sich gegenseitig die Fragen aus Übung 9.

2 Zeichnen Sie für Ihren Partner / Ihre Partnerin den Tagesablauf wie im folgenden Beispiel.

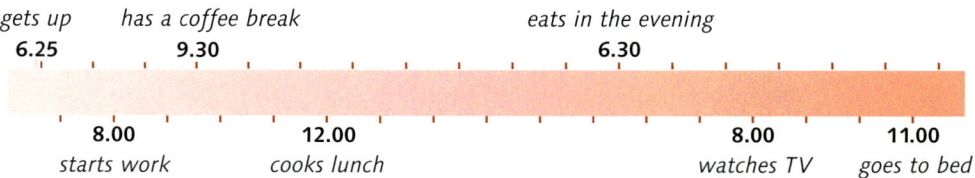

gets up   has a coffee break   eats in the evening
6.25   9.30   6.30

8.00   12.00   8.00   11.00
starts work cooks lunch   watches TV goes to bed

3 Erklären Sie einigen anderen Kursmitgliedern Ihre Zeichnung.

Useful language

(Petra) gets up at …
(She doesn't go out to work.)
(But she has children, so she starts work at home at … .)
(She doesn't usually have breakfast. She doesn't have time.)
After that …
Then …

I can ...

Bewerten Sie Ihren Lernerfolg. Ergänzen Sie.

Folgende Wörter, die ich gelernt habe, sind mir wichtig.

_____

_____

_____

_____

_____

Ich kann:
– meinen Tagesablauf beschreiben.

    I get up at _____

    _____.

    I (don't) have breakfast (at _____ *).*

    I _____.

    I _____

    _____.

    I go to bed at _____.

– jemanden fragen, wie sein Tagesablauf ist.

    When do _____ *?*

    _____ *?*

    And when do you _____

    _____ *?*

Außerdem kann ich Folgendes richtig anwenden:

• *Häufigkeitswörter wie always, usually, often*

My page 7

Culture link

Die normale Arbeitswoche für Angestellte in Großbritannien hat 40,5 Stunden. Pro Jahr erhält man 20–25 Urlaubstage, das ist etwas weniger als der europäische Durchschnitt. In den USA erhalten Angestellte am Anfang sogar nur 10 Urlaubstage pro Jahr, und müssen sich das Recht auf weitere Tage über die Jahre erarbeiten.

1 38 **Charlie's day**

a *Sally fragt Charlie über seinen Tagesablauf aus. Schreiben Sie ihre Fragen in voller Länge, dann hören Sie zu und kontrollieren Sie.*

When/you get up?
You/eat breakfast?
When/you start work?
You/have lunch?
You/cook in the evening?
What time/you go to bed?

At six.
No, I don´t.
At nine.
Yes, I do.
Not always.
At eleven.

b *Ergänzen Sie die Sätze über Charlie.*

1 Charlie gets up at _____.

2 He _____.

3 He _____.

4 He _____.

5 He _____.

6 He _____.

2 39 **Sally's day**

Hören Sie Sally zu, die jetzt von ihrem Tagesablauf erzählt und ordnen Sie die Uhrzeiten den Bildern zu.

a

c

e

b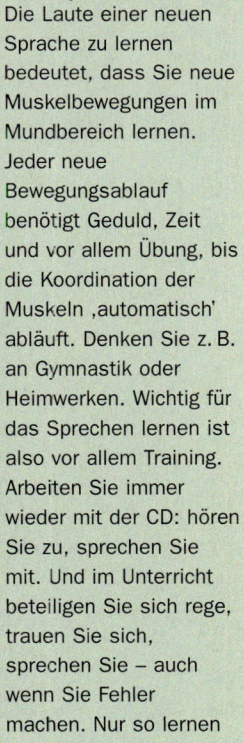

d

f

So trainieren Sie Ihre Aussprache

Die Laute einer neuen Sprache zu lernen bedeutet, dass Sie neue Muskelbewegungen im Mundbereich lernen. Jeder neue Bewegungsablauf benötigt Geduld, Zeit und vor allem Übung, bis die Koordination der Muskeln ‚automatisch' abläuft. Denken Sie z. B. an Gymnastik oder Heimwerken. Wichtig für das Sprechen lernen ist also vor allem Training. Arbeiten Sie immer wieder mit der CD: hören Sie zu, sprechen Sie mit. Und im Unterricht beteiligen Sie sich rege, trauen Sie sich, sprechen Sie – auch wenn Sie Fehler machen. Nur so lernen Sie Englisch zu sprechen.

3 **always, never, often, sometimes, usually**

a *Tragen Sie die Wörter an der richtigen Stelle ein.*

1	2	3	4	5
always				
100%	75%	50%	25%	0

b *Bilden Sie Sätze.*

1 I / have breakfast (0%)

2 She / cooks lunch / at 12 o'clock (50%)

3 Tom / doesn't start work / at 8.30 (75%)

4 We / have lunch in a café (25%)

5 They / don't work in the evening (50%)

6 Paul / has a break / at 11 o'clock (100%)

8 Free time

Talking about free time activities • Saying what there is in your town and what you can do there • Time adverbials with *every* • *there is* • *can/can't*

Focus 1 *What I do & how often*

go to a movie

go to a gym

go shopping

go for a walk

go swimming

Speaking

Pair work

1 Ask and answer.

Wie oft gehen Sie, den dargestellten Hobbys nach? Gibt es etwas, was Sie mit Ihrem Partner / Ihrer Partnerin gemeinsam haben?

> I sometimes go for a walk on Sunday afternoon. What about you?

> Me too!

> I never go to a gym.

> Me neither!

Remember

		always		**in**	the morning/afternoon/evening.
		usually		**in**	the week.
I	(don't)	**often**	go for a walk	**at**	(one) o'clock.
		sometimes		**at**	the weekend.
		never		**on**	(Sun)day (morning/afternoon/evening).
				on	a weekday.

Reading **2** ## Look and answer.

Sehen Sie sich den Cartoon an. Was antwortet Desmond?

Grammar

I	(don't)	go for a walk	**every morning/afternoon/evening/day.**
			every (Fri)day (morning/afternoon/evening).
			every weekday/weekend.

Practice **3** ## Read and decide.

Ist die Stellung der kursiv *gedruckten Ausdrücke richtig* (right) *oder falsch* (wrong)?
Korrigieren Sie die falschen Sätze.

       ✓   ✗

1 ☐ ☐ Desmond doesn't *usually* go to the gym.

2 ☐ ☐ The other man does *every day* sport.

3 ☐ ☐ Desmond watches *usually* TV *in the evening.*

4 ☐ ☐ He watches *every day* soap operas.

5 ☐ ☐ He *sometimes* watches breakfast TV *at the weekend.*

6 ☐ ☐ He *usually* gets up late *on Monday morning.*

7 ☐ ☐ Desmond plays *never* tennis.

8 ☐ ☐ He *sometimes* goes swimming.

9 ☐ ☐ He goes *every weekend* for a walk.

10 ☐ ☐ And he plays *every Sunday evening* cards with friends.

sixty-one   61

Pre-task

Pair work

4 ## Ask and answer.

Stellen Sie Fragen und finden Sie heraus, was Ihr Partner / Ihre Partnerin in der Freizeit macht. Machen Sie sich Notizen.

talk shows   football

WATCH

Hollywood films

cards   tennis

PLAY

computer games

to the sauna   to a gym

GO

to bed late

a newspaper   a magazine

READ

a book

Sauna: not often
Swimming: every weekend

> How often do you go to the sauna?

> Not often. But I go swimming every weekend.

Mini-task

5 ## Make a mini-profile of your partner.

1 *Schreiben Sie fünf Sätze darüber, was Ihr Partner / Ihre Partnerin wie oft macht auf einen Zettel.*
2 *Geben Sie den Zettel dem Kursleiter / der Kursleiterin.*
3 *Der Kursleiter / Die Kursleiterin liest einige Zettel vor. Die Klasse rät, wer gemeint ist.*

My partner goes for a walk with her dog every day.
She doesn't go swimming, but she often watches sport on TV.
She goes shopping every Thursday evening.
She doesn't often go to bed late, and she never sleeps in the afternoon.
She goes to the sauna every week.

Useful language

(I think) That's (Susanne).
No, it's not me.
(Birgit,) is it you?
Yes, it's me.

Focus 2 *Our town*

Vocabulary **6** ## Look and match.

Die Symbole stehen für Geschäfte, Einrichtungen usw., die es in einer Stadt gibt.
Ordnen Sie die Symbole den Begriffen im Kasten zu.

☐ bank	☐ cinema	☐ park	☐ sauna	☐ station
☐ bus stop	☐ gym	☐ post office	☐ school	☐ supermarket
☐ café	☐ hotel	☐ restaurant	☐ sports centre	☐ swimming pool

Listening **7** **40** ## Listen and decide.

Auf der CD spricht eine Frau über den Stadtteil, in dem sie wohnt. Welche der Geschäfte, Einrichtungen usw. aus Übung 6 werden genannt?

Now listen again and complete.

Hören Sie das Gespräch noch einmal an und ergänzen Sie diese Sätze.

There is a _____ only five minutes from the house.
And there's a _____ only 200 metres away.
There's a _____ too.
And there's a nice _____.
And there's a _____.
There isn't a _____.

Grammar ☞ p. 76

+	–	?
There's a shop.	**There isn't** a gym.	**Is there** a cinema?
		– Yes, **there is**. / No, **there isn't**.

Speaking **8** **Ask your teacher.**

Whole class

Wo wohnt Ihr Kursleiter / Ihre Kursleiterin? Stellen Sie Fragen.

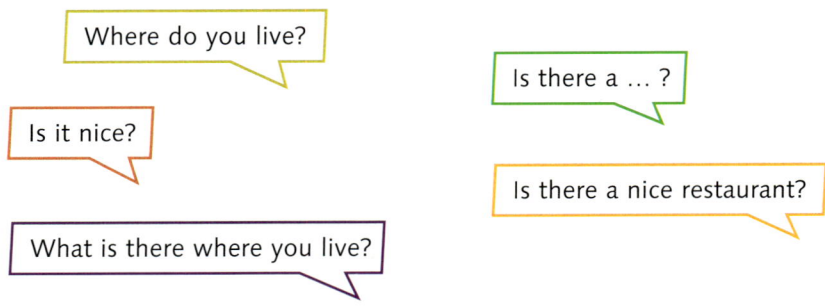

Where do you live?

Is there a … ?

Is it nice?

Is there a nice restaurant?

What is there where you live?

Pair work **Now talk to a partner.**

Erzählen Sie, wo Sie wohnen, und was es dort gibt. Stellen Sie Rückfragen. Machen Sie sich Notizen über den Wohnort Ihres Partners / Ihrer Partnerin.

Sonja:
Park: ✔
Cinema: ✘

Focus 3 *What I can and can't do*

Speaking **9** **Tell the class.**

In Übung 8 haben Sie herausgefunden, was es bei Ihrem Partner / Ihrer Partnerin in der Nähe gibt. Berichten Sie der Klasse, was er/sie dort unternehmen kann.

go for a walk	go to the gym	eat in a nice restaurant
go jogging	go to the sauna	play tennis
go swimming	go shopping	…
go to a movie	drink in nice bars	…

My partner (Sonja) lives in (Flensburg).
There's a nice (park), and she can (go for a walk or go jogging.)
And she can …
But she can't …

Grammar 📖 p. 76

I/You/He/She/It/We/You/They **can** swim.
I/You/He/She/It/We/You/They **can't** (= cannot) swim.

Can I/you/he/she/it/we/you/they swim? – Yes, I/… **can**. // No, I/… **can't**.

Pronunciation 10 ㊶ **Listen and decide.**

Was hören Sie jeweils im Satz: can *oder* can't*? Kreuzen Sie an.*

	can	can't			can	can't
1	☐	☐		**4**	☐	☐
2	☐	☐		**5**	☐	☐
3	☐	☐		**6**	☐	☐

㊷ **Now listen and repeat.**

Pre-task 11 **Look and write.**

Schreiben Sie, was Sie können und was Sie nicht können.

> swim ● swim 500 metres ● drive
> drive a bus ● play tennis ● play *Doppelkopf*
> use a mobile phone ● use a computer

> I can swim. But I can't swim 500 metres.

Mini-task 12 **Make a profile of your group.**

Pair work

1 *Stellen Sie sich gegenseitig Fragen zu den Stichwörtern in Übung 11.*

> Can you swim?

> Yes, I can.

> Can you swim 500 metres?

> No, I can't.

2 *Berichten Sie dem Kurs.*

Useful language

*Three people in our group can swim, and one can't.
Nobody in our group can swim 500 metres.*

Game 13 **Play the board game on pages 66 and 67.**

Group work

Regeln

1 Spielen Sie in Gruppen von drei oder vier Personen. Jedes Gruppenmitglied wählt eine Farbe und einen Anfangsstartpunkt.

2 Benutzen Sie eine Münze als Würfel.

= Rücken Sie ein Feld vor.
Go forward one space.

= Rücken Sie zwei Felder vor.
Go forward two spaces.

3 Lesen Sie die Frage für das Feld, auf dem Sie gelandet sind. Beantworten Sie sie. Wenn Sie mit *Yes, I …* antworten, liefern Sie anschließend den Beweis, indem Sie z.B. singen, oder das Wort bzw. die gewünschte Information nennen!

4 Wenn Sie mit *Yes, I …* antworten und den Beweis liefern, rücken Sie ein Feld vor – ohne auf dem neuen Feld noch einmal eine Aufgabe erfüllen zu müssen.
Wenn Sie mit *No, I …* antworten, bleiben Sie bis zur nächsten Runde auf dem Feld stehen.

5 Sieger/in ist, wer zuerst *The End* erreicht.

Useful language

It's your turn.
Can I have the coin, please?
Here you are.
Go forward one space/two spaces.
You're on number six now.
What does it say?

The 'can do' game
START

1 Can you sing an English song?
2 Do you know the name of Bart Simpson's sister?
3 Go forward one space.
4 Can you name a French film star?
5 Can you name two rooms in your home?
6 Can you say 'please' in Italian?
7 Miss a turn.
8 Do you know a city in Japan?
9 Can you name two days of the week?
10 Can you say two sentences about the teacher?

The 'can do' game
START

1 Do you know a nice restaurant here?
2 Can you say 'thank you' in Russian?
3 Go forward one space.
4 Can you name an English city?
5 Can you say what time it is now?
6 Miss a turn.
7 Do you know an American magazine?
8 Can you count from 1–20?
9 Can you say the names of three meals in English?
10 Can you sing a German song?

The 'can do' game

The 'can do' game
START

1 Can you say a sentence about your family?
2 Can you say 'goodbye' in Italian?
3 Can you say the names of the days at the weekend?
4 Do you know the name of the American president's husband/wife?
5 Miss a turn.
6 Can you sing an American song?
7 Can you name two drinks?
8 Go forward one space.
9 Can you name two places in a town?
10 Do you know who Charles and Elizabeth are?

The 'can do' game
START

1 Can you name two pets?
2 Do you know the names of two English football teams?
3 Miss a turn.
4 Can you sing 'Happy Birthday'?
5 Can you count from 21–30?
6 Do you know what day it is today?
7 Go forward one space.
8 Can you say four family words like 'daughter'?
9 Can you say 'no' in Spanish?
10 Can you name a city in Canada?

THE END

I can ...

Bewerten Sie Ihren Lernerfolg. Ergänzen Sie.

Folgende Wörter, die ich gelernt habe, sind mir wichtig.

_____
_____
_____
_____
_____

Ich kann:
– sagen, was ich in meiner Freizeit mache und wie oft. Ich kann auch entsprechende Fragen an andere stellen.

I _____
_____
_____
_____ .

– sagen, was es an meinem Wohnort bzw. bei mir in der Nähe (nicht) gibt.

There is _____
_____ .

There isn't _____
_____ .

– sagen, was ich kann und nicht kann.

I can _____ .

I can't _____ .

Außerdem kann ich Folgendes richtig anwenden:

• *Ausdrücke der Zeit wie every week, every Thursday*
• *there is*
• *can und can't*

❶ What we do

Ordnen Sie die Wörter den richtigen Wortspinnen zu. Manche Wörter passen zu mehr als einer Wortspinne. Fallen Ihnen noch mehr Wörter ein?

a book ● computer games ● films ● football ● to the gym ● a magazine
a newspaper ● to a restaurant ● ~~to the sauna~~ ● soap operas ● talk shows ● tennis

❷ Questions, questions, questions

a *Bilden Sie Fragen mit dem Verb* can *und die passenden Kurzantworten.*

Example: you / speak English? – Yes.
Can you speak English? – Yes, I can.

1 Irene / swim? – No.
2 Bill and Patsy / use a computer? – Yes.
3 they / play tennis? – No.
4 you / use a mobile phone? – Yes.

b *Bilden Sie Fragen mit dem Verb* do *und die passenden Kurzantworten.*

Example: you / like beer? – No.
Do you like beer? – No, I don't.

1 You / know Lucy? – Yes.
2 Barbara / watch TV every day? – No.
3 Sarah and Tom / have a car? – No.
4 We / speak English in class? – Yes.

c *Bilden Sie Fragen mit* Is there *und die passenden Kurzantworten.*

Example: a nice café where you live? – Yes.
Is there a nice café where you live? – Yes, there is.

1 a bank in this street? – No.
2 good boutique here? – Yes.
3 an Italian restaurant where you live? – No.
4 a café in your town? – No.

❸ My Town

43 *In seiner täglichen Radiosendung* My Town *befragt Peter Green Menschen zu ihrem Wohnort. In welcher Stadt befindet er sich heute?*

Newbridge   Falkirk   Hollyford

1 Vocabulary

8 points

Your score

8

Tragen Sie die Wörter und Wendungen in die Tabelle ein.

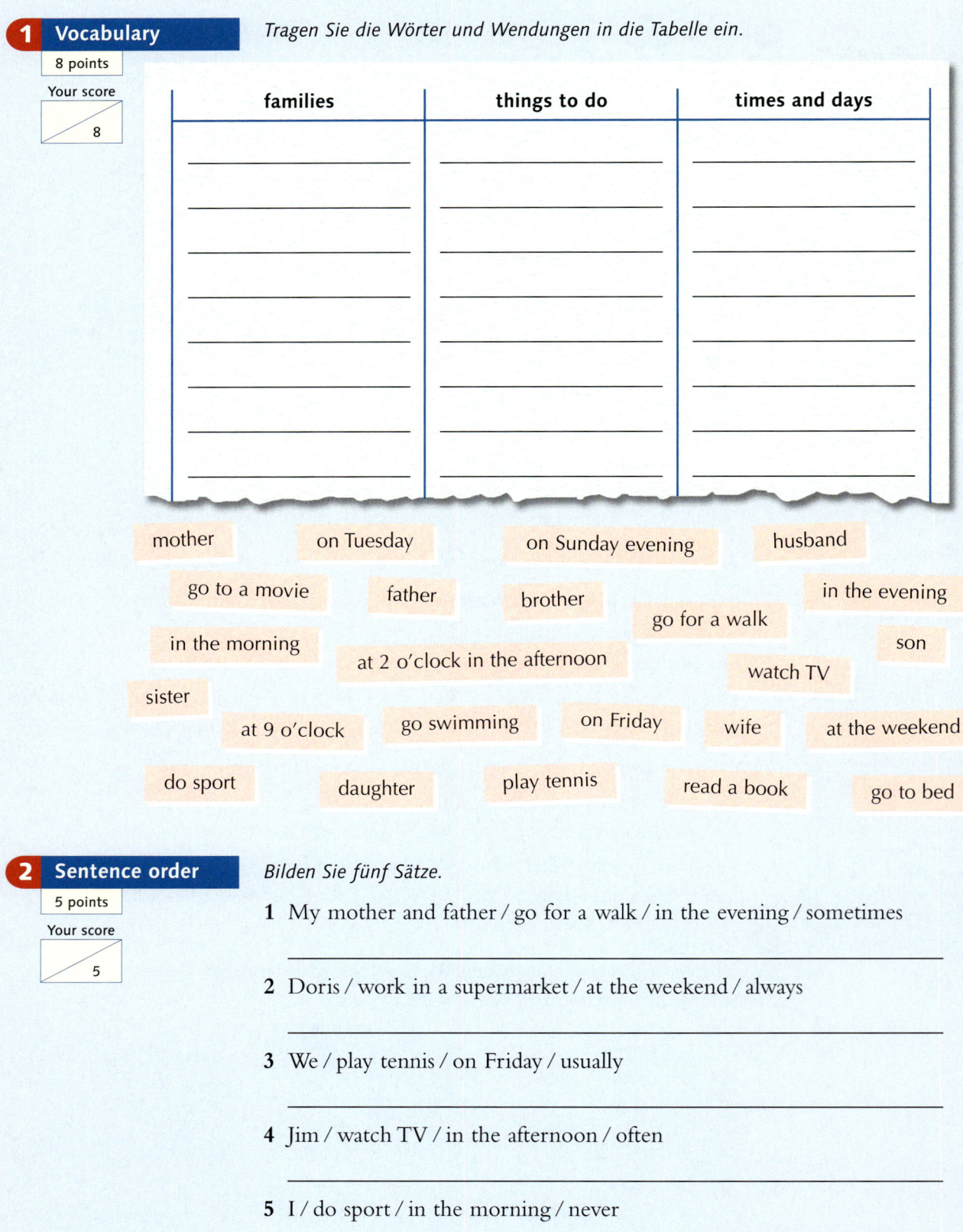

families	things to do	times and days
_____	_____	_____
_____	_____	_____
_____	_____	_____
_____	_____	_____
_____	_____	_____
_____	_____	_____
_____	_____	_____

mother   on Tuesday   on Sunday evening   husband

go to a movie   father   brother   in the evening

go for a walk

in the morning   son

at 2 o'clock in the afternoon   watch TV

sister

at 9 o'clock   go swimming   on Friday   wife   at the weekend

do sport   daughter   play tennis   read a book   go to bed

2 Sentence order

5 points

Your score

5

Bilden Sie fünf Sätze.

1 My mother and father / go for a walk / in the evening / sometimes

_____

2 Doris / work in a supermarket / at the weekend / always

_____

3 We / play tennis / on Friday / usually

_____

4 Jim / watch TV / in the afternoon / often

_____

5 I / do sport / in the morning / never

_____

3 Listening 44

10 points

Your score

10

Hören Sie Jenny und Mark zu und beantworten Sie die Fragen.

1 Is Mark always late on a Monday morning?
_____^{1}, he _____^{2}

2 When does he go to bed on Sunday evening?
He _____ ^{3}

3 When does Jenny get up on Saturday and Sunday morning?
On Saturday she _____^{4} and on Sunday she _____^{5}

4 Where does she go on Saturday evenings?
She _____ ^{6}

5 What does she do on Sunday?
She _____^{7} and _____^{8}

6 What does Mark usually do at the weekend?
He _____^{9} and _____^{10}

4 they're / their / there

6 points

Your score

6

Setzen Sie das richtige Wort ein.

1 _____^{1} is a nice café near here.

2 _____^{2} name is Brown.

3 _____^{3} good swimmers.

4 Is _____^{4} a hotel in your street?

5 _____^{5} isn't a sports centre in our town.

6 Laura and Tom have two children. – Are _____^{6} children at school?

5 Reading

6 points

Your score

6

Lesen Sie den Text über einen Englischkurs. Entscheiden Sie dann, ob die Sätze 1–6 richtig (✓) oder falsch (✗) sind. Korrigieren Sie die falschen Aussagen.

'I go to an English class on Thursday. It starts at 8.00 p.m. The teacher's name is Chris. She's from Scotland. Her husband is German. She's nice and the people in the class are nice, too. The class finishes at 9.30 and then we usually go to a café and talk English.'

	True	False
1 The English class starts at 8.00 in the morning.	☐	☐
2 The teacher is a man.	☐	☐
3 He/She is from Germany.	☐	☐
4 The teacher is married.	☐	☐
5 At 9.30 the people in the class usually go to a restaurant.	☐	☐
6 They never talk English after the class.	☐	☐

Total score

35

Grammatikübersicht

Inhalt

1 Grammatische Terminologie

Begriffe	Erklärung	Beispiele
Artikel Article	Artikel sind kleine Wörter, die vor (Adjektiv +) Nomen stehen.	der/die/das the ein/eine a/an
Bejaht Positive	Ein Satz oder eine Verbform ist bejaht, wenn er/sie eine positive Aussage hat und nicht ein Wort wie „nicht" oder „kein" enthält.	Serena likes her job. Serena mag ihre Arbeit.
Fürwort ⇢ Pronomen		
Genitiv Genitive	Die Genitivform eines Nomens zeigt ein Besitz- oder Zugehörigkeitsverhältnis an.	Bernds Tochter Bernd's daughter das Ende des Buches the end of the book
Geschlechtswort ⇢ Artikel		
Hauptwort ⇢ Nomen		
Häufigkeitsadverbien Adverbs of frequency	Häufigkeitsadverbien drücken aus, wie oft etwas geschieht.	manchmal sometimes Always immer
Nomen Noun	Nomen sind Bezeichnungen für Personen und Sachen.	Kursleiterin teacher Buch book
Possessivbegleiter Possessive determiner	Possessivbegleiter zeigen Zugehörigkeit an und beantworten die Frage „wessen?"	dein Buch your book unser Klassenzimmer our classroom
Pronomen Pronoun	Ein Pronomen steht an Stelle eines Nomens.	sie an Stelle von die Kursleiterin she instead of the teacher sie an Stelle von die Stadt it instead of the town
Substantiv ⇢ Nomen		
Tätigkeitswort ⇢ Verb		
Verb Verb	Das Verb ist meistens der Kern eines Satzes; es ist das Wort, das uns sagt, was getan wird. Verben drücken eine Handlung, einen Vorgang oder einen Zustand aus.	gehen go wohnen live mögen like
Verneint, Verneinung Negative	Ein Satz oder eine Verbform ist verneint, wenn er/sie eine negative Aussage hat und ein Wort wie „nicht" oder „kein" enthält.	Er hat keine Zeit. He doesn't have time. Sie ist nicht oft zu Hause. She's not often at home.
Zeitwort ⇢ Verb		

2 Das Nomen | The noun

2.1 Die Mehrzahl von Nomen | The plural of nouns

one sister – two sister**s** one book – two book**s**	one bus – two bus**es** one sandwich – two sandwich**es**	one child – two **children**

- Die Mehrzahl bildet man in aller Regel einfach durch Anhängen von **s**.
- Das **s** spricht man in der Regel als [z] aus, jedoch als [s] nach einem stimmlosen Laut wie **p**, **t**, **k**, **f**.
- Die Schreibweise einiger Nomen verändert sich.
  - Bei Nomen mit Endung **s**, **ss**, **sh**, **ch** oder **x** wird zusätzlich **e** eingefügt (bus – bus**es**)
    Dieses **e** spricht man als [ɪ] bus [bʌs] bus**es** [bʌsɪz] aus.
  - Bei Nomen mit der Endung Konsonant + **y** wird **y** zu **ie** (nationalit**y** – nationalit**ies**).
- Einige wenige Nomen haben Sonderformen in der Mehrzahl, z. B. **children**.

2.2 Das Genitiv *'s* | The genitive *'s*

Ann**'s** sister Anns Schwester	the driver's name *der Name des Fahrers*

- Besitz und Zugehörigkeit zeigt man wie im Deutschen durch Anhängen von **s** an – jedoch zusätzlich mit Apostroph.
- Nicht verwechseln:
  - Genitiv **'s**: Pat**'s** partner *Pats Partner*
  - **'s** als Kurzform von *is*: Pat**'s** from London. = *Pat ist aus London.*
- Bei Sachen zeigt man Zugehörigkeit meist mit **of** an: the end **of** the film = das Ende vom Film.

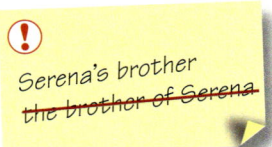

3 Die Artikel *a – an* und *the* | The articles *a – an* and *the*

vor Konsonant (Mitlaut)	*ein Kursleiter / eine Kursleiterin*	*der Kursleiter / die Kursleiterin*
vor Vokal (Selbstlaut)	an [ən] English teacher	the [ði:] English teacher

- Die Aussprache des nachfolgenden Wortes (nicht dessen Schreibweise) bestimmt Form und Aussprache des Artikels.
  - vor Konsonant: **a** [ə]
  - vor Vokal: **an** [ən], **the** [ði:]
  Besonderheiten des Artikelgebrauchs:
  - Berufsangaben mit Artikel: She's **a** teacher.
  - Kein Artikel bei **on** + Wochentag: on Monday
  - Kein Artikel bei go to work, go home, go to bed, have lunch usw.

4 Die Pronomen | The pronouns

4.1 *I/my, you/your, he/his …*

Wer?		Wessen?	
I	ich	my	mein
you	du/Sie	your	dein/Ihr
he	er	his	sein
she	sie	her	ihr
it	es	its	sein
we	wir	our	unser
you	ihr/Sie	your	euer/Ihr
they	sie	their	ihr

- Englisch macht keinen Unterschied zwischen „du/ihr" und „Sie": immer heißt es **you**.
- **I** schreibt man immer groß.
- Die Possessivbegleiter („Wessen?") sind unveränderlich – statt z. B. „mein/meine/meinen/meinem/meiner/meines" heißt es immer einfach **my**.

4.2 *this – that*

This is my friend, Alan. dies (hier), diese(r/s) (hier)	Who is **that** person there? das (da), jene(r/s) (da)

- Mit **this** verweist man auf etwas näher Liegendes.
- Mit **that** verweist man auf etwas entfernt Liegendes.

5 Das Verb | The verb

5.1 Die einfache Gegenwart des Verbs *be* | The simple present of the verb *be*

Aussage	Frage		Kurzantworten	
I**'m (not)** = I **am (not)** late.	**Am** I	late?	Yes, I am.	No, I**'m not**.
You**'re (not)** = You **are (not)** late.	**Are** you	late?	Yes, you **are**.	No, you**'re not**.
He**'s (not)** = He **is (not)** late.	**Is** he	late?	Yes, he **is**.	No, he**'s not**.
She**'s (not)** = She **is (not)** late.	**Is** she	late?	Yes, she **is**.	No, she**'s not**.
It**'s (not)** = It **is (not)** late.	**Is** it	late?	Yes, it **is**.	No, it**'s not**.
We**'re (not)** = We **are (not)** late.	**Are** we	late?	Yes, we **are**.	No, we**'re not**.
You**'re (not)** = You **are (not)** late.	**Are** you	late?	Yes, you **are**.	No, you**'re not**.
They**'re (not)** = They **are (not)** late.	**Are** they	late?	Yes, they **are**.	No, they**'re not**.

- Die Kurzformen **'m**, **'re**, und **'s** stehen für **am**, **are** und **is**. Kurzformen sind in der gesprochenen Sprache üblich.
- Die Verneinung bildet man auf zweierlei Art:
  – Kurzform (**'m**, **'s**, **'re**) + **not**
  – Vollform mit direkt angehängtem **n't**: you/we/they **aren't**, he/she/it **isn't**
  Ausnahme: zu **I am** gibt es nur eine verneinte Form: **I'm not**.

5.2 Die einfache Gegenwart anderer Verben | The simple present of other verbs

Bejaht	Verneint	Frage	Kurzantworten
I/We/You/They **work**.	I/We/You/They **don't work**.	**Do** I/we/you/they **work**?	Yes, I/we/you/they **do**. No, I/we/you/they **don't**.
He/She/It **works**.	He/She/It **doesn't work**.	**Does** he/she/it **work**?	Yes, he/she/it **does**. No, he/she/it **doesn't**.

- In bejahten Sätzen wird nach **he**, **she**, **it** (und Ausdrücken, die durch **he**, **she** oder **it** ersetzt werden könnten) **s** an die Grundform des Verbs angehängt.
  Schreibbesonderheiten:
  – Nach **ss**, **sh**, **ch** oder **x** wird zusätzlich **e** eingefügt: fini**sh** – finish**es**, wat**ch** – wat**ch**es.
  – Einige wenige Verben haben Sonderformen: **has**, **goes**, **does**.
- In verneinten Sätzen, Fragen und Kurzantworten wird **do** oder **does** eingesetzt:
  – I, you, we, they: **do(n't)**
  – he, she, it: **does(n't)**.

5.3 *can*

Bejaht	I/You/He/She/It/We/You/They **can** swim.
Verneint	I/You/He/She/It/We/You/They **can't** (= **cannot**) swim.
Frage	**Can** I/you/he/she/it/we/you/they swim?
Kurzantworten	Yes, I/... **can**. / No, I/... **can't**.

- **can** (können) und die verneinte Form **can't** (Vollform: **cannot**) sind für alle Personen gleich.

5.4 *there is*

Bejaht	**There's** = **There is** a gym. Es gibt ein Fitnessstudio.
Verneint	**There's not** = **There isn't** a café. Es gibt kein Café.
Frage	**Is there** a shop? Gibt es ein Geschäft?
Kurzantworten	Yes, **there is**. Ja, das gibt es. No, **there isn't**. Nein, das gibt es nicht.

- **there is** entspricht „es gibt" im Deutschen.

6 Häufigkeitsadverbien | Adverbs of frequency

Häufigkeitsadverbien drücken aus, wie oft etwas geschieht. Sie stehen meist nach dem Pronomen und vor dem Verb.

> I **sometimes** sleep late on Saturdays. Samstags schlafe ich manchmal länger.
> We **never** go to the gym in the morning. Morgens gehen wir nie ins Fitnessstudio.
> I **often** read the newspaper at the weekend. Am Wochenende lese ich oft die Zeitung.
> They **always** eat salad for lunch. Mittags essen sie immer Salat.

Transcript

Dialoge, die im Kursbuch abgedruckt sind, werden nicht im Transcript aufgeführt.

(02) Unit 1 Exercise 2

LOLA   Hello. Hello. Hello. Hello. Ah! Hello and welcome. I'm Lola. And this is Tony. I'm your guide on ...

(07) My page 1 Exercise 2

1

WOMAN   Hello. I'm Barbara.

MAN   Nice to meet you, Barbara. I'm Andreas and this is Helmut.

2

MAN   Who's that?

WOMAN   Sorry, I don't know.

CHILD   It's the clown!

3

MAN   Nice to meet you, Laura.

WOMAN   Nice to meet you too, Jack. Welcome to CRS.

(10) Unit 2 Exercise 3

A   What's your name, please?

B   Lindsey.

A   Is that your first name?

B   No, it's my surname. My first name is Pat.

A   So you're Pat Lindsey.

B   Yes, that's right.

A   Can you write that, please?

(14) My page 2 Exercise 2

MAN   What's your name?

WOMAN   Lilo.

MAN   What's your surname?

WOMAN   Schmidt.

MAN   Is that your husband?

WOMAN   Yes. His name's Olaf.

MAN   Who's that?

WOMAN   That's my business partner, Heinrich, and his family.

(15) Unit 3 Exercise 1

It's been a hard day's night, and I've been working like a dog

It's been a hard day's night, I should be sleeping like a log

But when I get home to you I find the things that you do

Will make me feel all right.

You know I work all day to get you money to buy you things

And it's worth it just to hear you say you're going to give me everything

So why on earth should I moan, 'cause when I get you alone

You know I feel ok.

When I'm home, everything seems to be right

When I'm home, feeling you holding me tight, tight, yeah

It's been a hard day's night, and I've been working like a dog

It's been a hard day's night, I should be sleeping like a log

But when I get home to you I find the things that you do

Will make me feel all right. ...

... The taxman's taken all my dough and left me in my stately home

lazing on a sunny afternoon.

And I can't sail my yacht, he's taken everything I've got

all I've got's this sunny afternoon.

Save me, save me, save me from this squeeze

I've got a big fat momma trying to break me.

And I love to live so pleasantly, live this life of luxury

lazing on a sunny afternoon

in the summertime

in the summertime

in the summertime

My girlfriend's gone off with my car and gone back to her ma and pa

telling tales of drunkenness and cruelty.

Now I'm sitting here, sipping at my ice-cold beer

lazing on a sunny afternoon.

(16) Unit 3 Exercise 2

WAITER   Morning.

WOMAN   Good morning.

WAITER   How are you this morning?

WOMAN   Not so bad, thanks. And you?

WAITER   I'm fine, thanks. What's your room number, please?

WOMAN   Six oh seven.

(20) My page 3 Exercise 2

1

MAN   What's Christa's number?

WOMAN   It's oh, one, two, three, four, five, six, seven, eight, nine.

MAN   Oh, one, two, three, four, five, six, seven, eight, nine?

WOMAN   That's right.

2

MAN   What's Doro's number?

WOMAN   It's oh, three, oh, four, nine, two, five, eight, five, four.

MAN	Oh, three, oh, four, nine, two, five, eight, five, four. Thanks.

3

MAN	What's Isobel's mobile number?
WOMAN	It's oh, one, four, two, three, nine, six, eight, seven, five.
MAN	That's oh, one, four, two, three, nine, six, eight ... ?
WOMAN	Seven, five.

4

MAN	What's Frank's number?
WOMAN	It's oh, seven, six, one, two, nine, five, two, six, oh.
MAN	Sorry? Can you say that again, please?
WOMAN	Oh, seven, six, one, two, nine, five, two, six, oh.
MAN	Thanks.

5

MAN	What's Gunther's mobile number?
WOMAN	It's oh, one, seven, nine, four, one, oh, nine, three, six, two.

6

MAN	What's Hannah's number?
WOMAN	It's oh, three, one, two, six, nine, five, oh, four, six.

(26) My page 4 Exercise 3

JIM	Do you have a TV?
MAY	No, I don't. I don't like TV.
JIM	No? I like TV. I have 60 channels.
MAY	Oh. I have a radio.
JIM	Do you like music?
MAY	Yes, I love classical music. I have a CD player and about 50 CDs. Do you like classical music?
JIM	No, I don't. I like pop music, but I don't like classical music. I don't have a CD player. I have a DVD player and 19 pop DVDs.
JIM	Do you have children?
MAY	No, I don't. Do you?
JIM	I have 30 children.
MAY	Thirty children!?
JIM	Yes, I have 30 children – in my kindergarten group.

(27) Quick check 1 Exercise 5

1

Oh, erm. Hello, my name is Ed. I like opera and I like good food and wine. And, erm I have a cat. My number is 0122 ...

2

This is Mary. You like jogging and fitness and you're interested in pop music. I like these things too! You have two children and a dog. That's OK for me. My telephone number is 0124 ...

(29) Unit 5 Exercise 12

WOMAN	Hello, what's your name?
CHILD	Caroline.
WOMAN	Hi, Caroline. I'm Ann. Is this your cat?
CHILD	Yes, her name is Mog.
CAT	Miaow.
WOMAN	She's nice.
CHILD	Mm.
WOMAN	Mog's a good name for a cat.
CHILD	Our other cats are Meg, Mollie and Mandy.
WOMAN	You have four cats?
CHILD	Mm.
WOMAN	Mog, Mel, Mollie and Mandy?
CHILD	No. Mog, Meg, Mollie and Mandy.
WOMAN	Right. Do you live here?
CHILD	Yes, I do.
WOMAN	And is your mum at home?
CHILD	Yes, she is.
WOMAN	Good. ... Hello, Mrs Thomas?
2ND WOMAN	Yes.
WOMAN	Hello. I'm Ann Baxter, Sam's colleague.
2ND WOMAN	Oh, yes, right. Yes, of course. Come in, please come in. Sam told me that ...

(30) My page 5 Exercise 2

MAN	Is this your family, Sarah?
WOMAN	Yes. This is my partner, Ken, and my son, Toby. That's Toby's wife, Lucy, and their baby, Valerie.
MAN	And who's that?
WOMAN	That's my sister, Marion.
MAN	And the girls? Are they your daughters?
WOMAN	No, they're Marion's daughters. Their names are Fiona and Lauren.
MAN	Nice names.
WOMAN	Yes.
MAN	And who's the woman with Ken?
WOMAN	That's Anna. She's Ken's daughter.
MAN	You really have a big family.
WOMAN	Hm. Yes, I do.

(31) Unit 6 Exercise 4

1

A	What time is it?
B	It's half past two.

2

C	Excuse me. What time is it, please?
D	Sorry, I don't know.
C	Oh, OK. ... Excuse me. What time is it, please?
E	It's quarter past ten.
C	Thanks.

3

F   Excuse me. What time is it, please?

G   It's half past three.

F   Three thirty?

G   Yes.

F   Thank you.

G   No problem.

4

Flight FM 3426 to Amsterdam will depart at 17.10 from Gate 25. Flight FM 3426 to Amsterdam will depart at 17.10 from Gate 25.

5

Flight SN 270 to Las Palmas will depart at 10.20 from Gate 12. Flight SN 270 to Las Palmas will depart at 10.20 from Gate 12.

(33) **Unit 6 Exercise 10**

Six o'clock already I was just in the middle of a dream
I was kissing Valentino by a crystal blue Italian stream
But I can't be late 'cause then I guess I just won't get paid
These are the days when you wish your bed was already made.
It's just another manic Monday
I wish it was Sunday
'Cause that's my fun day
My I don't have to run day
It's just another manic Monday.
Have to catch an early train, got to be at work by nine
And if I had an aeroplane, I still couldn't make it on time
'Cause it takes me so long just to figure out what I'm gonna wear
Blame it on the train but the boss is already there.
It's just another manic Monday
I wish it was Sunday
'Cause that's my fun day
My I don't have to run day
It's just another manic Monday.
All of my nights why did my lover have to pick last night to get down
Doesn't matter that I have to feed the both of us, employment's down
He tells me in his bedroom voice:
"C'mon honey, let's go make some noise"
Time, it goes so fast
It's just another manic Monday
I wish it was Sunday
'Cause that's my fun day
My I don't have to run day
It's just another manic Monday.

(34) **My page 6 Exercise 2**

1

MAN   What day do you go swimming, Pat?

WOMAN   I go on Monday, Wednesday and Thursday.

MAN   Oh.

2

WOMAN   What are your hobbies, Pierre?

MAN   I go to an English class.

WOMAN   Is it in the evening?

MAN   Yes. Tuesday and Friday evening.

3

MAN   Do you like sport, Carol?

WOMAN   Well, I play tennis.

MAN   Oh. Do you play at the sports club?

WOMAN   Yes. Do you go there too?

MAN   Yes. Can we have a game?

WOMAN   Hm. OK. I go there on Saturday, Sunday or Tuesday.

4

WOMAN   What sports do you do, Eric?

MAN   Bodybuilding on Thursday and gymnastics on Friday.

5

MAN   Do you go to the disco, Ellen?

WOMAN   Yes. On Saturday, Sunday and Thursday. It's oldies night on a Thursday.

MAN   Right.

6

WOMAN   When's your jazz dance class, John?

MAN   Erm. I go to three classes.

WOMAN   Three classes!?

MAN   Yes, Monday, Tuesday and Wednesday.

WOMAN   Hm.

(36) **Unit 7 Exercise 3**

A   So what do you do, Kim?

B   I'm a waitress. I work in a bistro.

A   Oh right. Tell me about your day.

B   Well, I start work at eleven thirty.

A   In the morning?

B   Yes. And I finish at half past two.

A   OK.

B   But I start again at six in the evening. And I don't finish before eleven.

A   That's a long day. You must go to bed late.

B   Yes, but I don't get up very early.

A   That's true. So you have a big break in the afternoon.

B   Yes, I do.

A   And what do you do then?

B   I go shopping, watch TV, go out with my dog.

A   I see. Do you work at the weekend too?

B   On Saturday, but not on Sunday.

A   So Sunday is your free day.

B   Yes.

A   And you, Christine? You're a systems administrator, is that right?

C   Yes, I'm one of a team. We work round the clock.

A   You work in a factory?

C   Yes. I work Monday to Friday, from six in the morning till two in the afternoon. My colleagues work the rest of the day, from two in the afternoon till ten at night.

A   So when do you get up?

C   At half past four in the morning.

A   Half past four?! You must go to bed early.

C   Yes, I do. At ten o'clock.

A   Right. Do you have breakfast at half past four?

C   No, not at half past four. I have a coffee break, and my breakfast, at nine o'clock.

A   So what do you do in the afternoon?

C   I go jogging.

A   Every day?

C   Yes, every day.

A   So you're very fit. Do you work at the weekends?

C   No, only Monday to Friday.

A   That's nice.

38 *My page 7* **Exercise 1**

SALLY   When do you get up?
CHARLIE   At six.
SALLY   Do you eat breakfast?
CHARLIE   No, I don't.
SALLY   When do you start work?
CHARLIE   At nine.
SALLY   Do you have lunch?
CHARLIE   Yes, I do.
SALLY   Do you cook in the evening?
CHARLIE   Not always.
SALLY   What time do you go to bed?
CHARLIE   At eleven.

39 *My page 7* **Exercise 2**

I like my job. I work in a hospital. I get up at seven o'clock. Then I go to the pub for a coffee and a sandwich. Then I go to work. I start at 10 in the evening and I finish at six in the morning. When I finish work, I go home, I have breakfast and go to bed.

40 **Unit 8** **Exercise 7**

A   Tell me, June. Where do you live? Do you live in the centre of town?

B   No, not in the centre. I'm 20 minutes from the centre.

A   Is it a nice part of town, do you like it?

B   Yes, it's a good place to live. There is a school only

five minutes from the house. And there's a supermarket only 200 metres away.

A   That's good.

B   There's a bank too.

A   A bank, mm.

B   Yes, and there's a nice Italian restaurant.

A   Italian. Nice.

B   And there's a sports centre, a sports centre with a swimming pool. I go there every morning.

A   Wow! Every morning?

B   Yes, when the children are at school.
    It's only ten minutes from the house, and there isn't a park where I can go jogging, so I go to the sports centre.

A   Right.

43 *My page 8* **Exercise 3**

INTERVIEWER   Today we're in the shopping centre in ... . Excuse me, do you live here in the town?
WOMAN   Yes, I do. I live in the town centre.
INTERVIEWER   Do you like it?
WOMAN   Oh, yes. It's very nice. There are nice shops and good restaurants. And there's a cinema and a theatre.
INTERVIEWER   Is ... a good place for children?
WOMAN   Well, there's a school and there's a park. The children can play in the park.
INTERVIEWER   And is there a sports centre?
WOMAN   No, there isn't. But there's a swimming pool in the park. That's very nice in summer. You can really relax there.

44 **Quick check 2** **Exercise 3**

JENNY   Hi, Mark. How are you?
MARK   OK.
JENNY   You're late. You're always late on a Monday morning.
MARK   Mm.
JENNY   When do you usually go to bed on Sunday?
MARK   One or two o'clock.
JENNY   One or two o'clock? I can't go to bed that late. I always get up at six in the week.
MARK   Six? Ugh. Do you get up later at the weekend?
JENNY   Well, I get up at eight on Saturday and on Sunday morning I get up at nine or ten. I like to relax at the weekend. I usually go to the disco on Saturday evening. On Sunday I go jogging and sometimes I play tennis in the afternoon. What about you? What do you do at the weekend?
MARK   I stay in bed.
JENNY   Huh? You stay in bed all weekend?
MARK   No, not all weekend. I go to the pub in the evening.

My page & Quick Check Key

My page 1 *page 11*

1 Across
  2 volleyball   **5** tennis   **8** jogging

  Down
  1 football   **3** badminton   **4** walking
  6 surfing   **7** hockey   **9** golf

2 1 I'm   **2** you   **3** this   **4** that   **5** I   **6** It
  7 Nice   **8** too   **9** Welcome

3 a 6   **b** 4   **c** 5   **d** 1   **e** 2   **f** 3

My page 2 *page 19*

1 2 name   **3** family   **4** are   **5** his   **6** married
  7 am   **8** husband   **9** her   **10** is   **11** single
  12 you   **13** surname   **14** my   **15** your

2 a 1 What's your name?   **b** d
    2 What's your surname?   c
    3 Is that your husband?   a
    4 Who's that?   b

3 1 What's Julie's surname?
  2 Where's she/Julie from?
  3 Where's her family from?
  4 What's her partner's name?
  5 Where's he/Tony from?
  6 Where's his family from?

Manfred Frey
Lösungsvorschlag

  1 What's Manfred's surname?   Frey.
  2 Where's he from?   Switzerland.
  3 Where's his family from?   Zürich.
  4 What's his partner's name?   Marta Dubow.
  5 Where's she from?   Hungary.
  6 Where's her family from?   Budapest.

4 Germany   Turkey   Spain   Portugal
  The Czech Republic   Russia   Poland
  Hungary   Croatia

My page 3 *page 27*

1
1 evening   **2** How   **3** fine
4 Good   **5** morning   **6** thanks

2 1 0123 456789   **2** 0304 925854
  3 01423 96875   **4** 0761 295260
  5 0179 4109362   **6** 0312 695046

3
Lösungsvorschlag

Tim is a good cook.
Gabi is an opera fan.
Tim is not a tennis fan.
Tim is a rock music fan.
Gabi is interested in horror films.
Tim is interested in golf.
Gabi is interested in the internet.

My page 4 *page 35*

1 a

  b **food**   hamburger   pizza
    drinks   beer   coffee
    pets   cat   dog
    children   daughter   son
    music   opera   pop
    sport   football   jogging

2 2 Do you like red wine?
  3 Do you have a dog?
  4 Do you like sport?
  5 Do you like computers?
  6 Do you have a car?

3 a Jim: TV; pop music; DVD player; children
    May: radio, classical; CD player
  b TV channels: 60
    CDs: 50
    DVDs: 19
    children: 30

Quick Check 1   *pages 36–37*

1 1 g   **2** h   **3** f   **4** b   **5** e   **6** a   **7** c   **8** d
2 1 am   **2** are   **3** are   **4** is   **5** Is   **6** aren't
  7 am; is   **8** aren't; are

3 Dialogue 1
2 It   3 your   4 your   5 Her   6 She
Dialogue 2
1 my   2 His   3 he   4 He   5 My
6 She   7 you

4 1 How   2 Who   3 Where   4 What
5 Who   6 What   7 Where   8 How

5 a
Paula: 0126
Ken: 0123
b
Paula: 0122
Ken: 0124

My page 5 *page 45*

1 a Across
4 husband
7 sister
8 partner
Down
1 father
2 wife
3 mother
5 brother
6 daughter
b Familienwort: **Married**

2 1 partner   2 husband and wife   3 daughter
4 sister   5 sisters   6 daughter

3 1 works   2 like   3 live   4 has
5 don't like   6 doesn't live
7 have   8 don't work

My page 6 *page 51*

1 2 Tuesday   3 Wednesday   4 Thursday
5 Friday   6 Saturday   7 Sunday

2 1 b   2 c   3 e   4 d   5 f   6 a

3 b
1 09:30: It's half past nine.
2 13:45: It's quarter to two.
3 20:15: It's quarter past eight.
4 11:30: It's half past eleven.

4 1 on   2 at   3 in   4 at   5 at   6 in
7 at   8 in

My page 7 *page 59*

1 a When do you get up?
Do you eat breakfast?
When do you start work?
Do you have lunch?
Do you cook in the evening?
What time do you go to bed?
b 1 Charlie gets up at six.
2 He doesn't eat breakfast.
3 He starts work at nine.
4 He has lunch.
5 He doesn't always cook in the evening.
6 He goes to bed at eleven.

2 a 4   **b** 3   **c** 2   **d** 6   **e** 5   **f** 1

3 a 2 usually   3 often
4 sometimes   5 never
b 1 I never have breakfast.
2 She often cooks lunch at 12 o'clock.
3 Tom doesn't usually start work at 8.30.
4 We sometimes have lunch in a café.
5 They don't often work in the evening.
6 Paul always has a break at 11 o'clock.

My page 8 *page 69*

1
Lösungsvorschlag
go
to the gym
to a restaurant
for a walk
jogging
shopping
read
a book
a magazine
a newspaper
watch
films / a movie
soap operas
talk shows
play
computer games
football
tennis
hockey

2 a 1 Can Irene swim? No, she can't.
   2 Can Bill and Patsy use a computer? Yes, they can.
   3 Can they play tennis? No, they can't.
   4 Can you use a mobile phone? Yes, I can.
   b 1 Do you know Lucy? Yes, I do.
   2 Does Barbara watch TV every day? No, she doesn't.
   3 Do Sarah and Tom have a car? No, they don't.
   4 Do we speak English in class? Yes, we do.
   c 1 Is there a bank in this street? No, there isn't.
   2 Is there an Italian restaurant where you live? No, there isn't.
   3 Is there a good boutique here? Yes, there is.
   4 Is there a café in your town? No, there isn't.

3 Peter is in Hollyford (the only town which has a swimming pool).

Quick Check 2   *pages 70–71*

1 families
mother
sister
father
daughter
brother
husband
wife
son

things to do
go to a movie
do sport
go swimming
go for a walk
play tennis
watch TV
read a book
go to bed

times and days
in the morning
at 9 o'clock
on Tuesday
at 2 o'clock in the afternoon
on Sunday evening
on Friday
in the evening
at the weekend

2 1 My mother and father sometimes go for a walk in the evening.
   2 Doris always works in a supermarket at the weekend.
   3 We usually play tennis on Friday.
   4 Jim often watches TV in the afternoon.
   5 I never do sport in the morning.

3 1 Yes
   2 is
   3 goes to bed at one or two o'clock.
   4 gets up at eight
   5 gets up at nine or ten.
   6 usually goes to the disco.
   7 goes jogging
   8 sometimes plays tennis.
   9 stays in bed.
   10 goes to the pub.

4 1 There
   2 Their
   3 They're
   4 there
   5 There
   6 their

5 1 False: the English class starts at 8.00 in the evening.
   2 False: the teacher is a woman.
   3 False: she's from Scotland.
   4 True.
   5 False: at 9.30 the people in the class usually go to a café.
   6 False: they (usually) talk English after the class.

Class List

Name	Phone number	Mobile number

First 1 Choice Englisch für Erwachsene

Starter Kursbuch

Im Auftrag des Verlages erarbeitet von	John Stevens, Bad Münstereifel, und Isobel Williams, Freiburg (My Pages und Quick Checks).
Beratende Mitarbeit	Astrid Hornoff, Leipzig; Christine House, Berlin; Isobel Williams, Freiburg
Redaktion	Sinéad Butler (verantwortliche Redakteurin), Christine House
Redaktionelle Mitarbeit	Sarah Smith, Stephanie Kramer
Bildredaktion	Suzanne Williams/Pictureresearch.co.uk
Projektleitung	Helga Holtkamp
Illustration	Oxford Designers & Illustrators: Kate Charlesworth, Mark Duffin, Gary Wing
Layout und technische Umsetzung	Oxford Designers & Illustrators
Umschlaggestaltung	Knut Waisznor
Umschlagfoto	ips, International Publishing Services für Cornelsen Verlag, © Cornelsen Verlag

Weitere Kursmaterialien

Teaching Guide
Extra Language Trainer mit CD-ROM

Bildquellen

Agentur Focus S.23/Vadystadt; **Alamy** S.29/Dave Porter, 38/wherrett.com, 38/Joe Soh, 52/Ilianski; **Axiom** S.20/Timothy Allen; **Capital Pictures** S.38, 39; **Comstock** S.19/Royalty-free; **Corel Library** S.15, 16/Royalty-free; **Corbis** S.8/Bettmann, 12/LWA-JDC, 20/J.P.Lescourret, 23/D. Raymer; **Empics** S.8/AP Photo/John F. Kennedy National Historic Site; **Flonline** S.14/A.Richter; **Getty Images** S.6/Antonio Mo, 8, 8/Time Life Pictures/Ed Clark/Stringer, 8/Hulton Archive, 8/Hulton Archive/Stringer, 16/D.Boyer, 14/Chabruken, 12/L.D. Gordon, 16/Nicole Duplaix, 16/Jerry Driendl, 20/J.Lamb/Royalty-free, 25/B.Slezak, 29/Robin MacDougall, 31/Photonica, 31/Mike Powell, 32/Mel Yates, 38/AFP, 38/Mike Hewitt, 38/Dennis O'Clair, 42/Yellow Dog Productions, 43/Stephen Simpson, 43/Alex Mares-Manton, 43/Catherine Ledner, 44/Microzoa, 46/Timothy Shonnard, 46/Stuart Hughs, 46/Erin Patrice O'Brien, 46/Andreas Pollok, 52/Peter Hince, 52/Ron Chapple, 54/Paul Thomas, 54/Seth Joel, 60/Jeff Smith, 60/GDT, 60/Photonica; **ifa-Bilderteam** S.19/J. Heron, 21/W. Grubb; **images.de** S23/Giribas; **The Kobal Collection** S.8/United Artists, 38; **Picture Alliance** S.16/obs; **Punchstock** S.6/Tim Hall Photodisc red, 22/Medioimages, 29/Goodshoot, 29/Stockdisc, 31/Ryan McVay/Photodisc green, 32/Inti St Clair/Photodisc Red, 32/Trinette Reed/Blend Images, 43/BananaStock, 46/John Dowland/Photoalto, 52/Andersen-Ross/Brand X, 60/Photodisc blue, 60/BananaStock; **Redferns Music Picture Gallery** S.23; **Rex Features** S.8/FTE, 8/Sipa Press, 8/Rex, 8/Mimmo Chanura (AGF), 8/Frank Rollitz (WSH), 8/Eric Vidal (SEN), 8/Snap (SYP); **Schapowalow** S.16/v.d Hecken/Heaton, 20/Atlantide; **Visum** S.16/Travel Ink; **Zefa Images** S.12/T. Pannell, 13/T. Pannell, 23/K.Solveig/C. Goerling.

www.cornelsen.de

Die Internetadressen und –dateien, die in diesem Lehrwerk angegeben sind, wurden vor Drucklegung geprüft. Der Verlag übernimmt keine Gewähr für die Aktualität und den Inhalt dieser Adressen und Dateien oder solcher, die mit ihnen verlinkt sind.

1. Auflage, 1. Druck 2005

Alle Drucke dieser Auflage sind inhaltlich unverändert und können im Unterricht nebeneinander verwendet werden.

© 2005 Cornelsen Verlag, Berlin

Druck: CS-Druck CornelsenStürtz, Berlin

ISBN-13: 978-3-464-01965-8

ISBN-10: 3-464-01965-9

Inhalt gedruckt auf säurefreiem Papier, umweltschonend hergestellt aus chlorfrei gebleichten Faserstoffen.

Audio CD

Aufnahmeleitung: Johan Nordqvist

Co-Produktion: Olaf Stemme

Toningenieur: Ed Epstein

Tontechnik: Nordqvist Produktions, Sweden (Head Office)

Verlagsredaktion: Sinéad Butler

Quellen:

Audioaufnahme: *Sunny Afternoon* (Raymond T. Davis) von dem Album *The Kinks - Hit Singles*, © 1987 PRT Records Ltd / Teldec Schallplatten GmbH; **Text: S. 77** *Sunny Afternoon* (Raymond T. Davis) © DAVRAY Music Ltd. / Carlin Music Corp. by permission of Greenhorn Musikverlag GmbH & Co. KG

Audioaufnahme: *A Hard Day's Night* (Lennon/McCartney) von dem Album *The Beatles* © 2000 EMI Records Ltd.; **Text: S. 77** *A Hard Day's Night* (Lennon/McCartney) © Sony/ATV Tunes LLC. Alle Rechte für Deutschland, Österreich und die Schweiz bei Sony/ATV Music Publishing (Germany) GmbH

Audioaufnahme: *Manic Monday* (Prince R. Nelson) von dem Album *Different Light* © 1985 Controversy Music; **Text: S. 80** *Manic Monday* (Prince R. Nelson) © Universal/MCA Publishing GmbH, Berlin

Sprecher/innen:
Laura Cameron
Peter Gilbert Cotton
Lucy Faith Cran
Marianne Graffam
Shaun Lawton
Catherine McNaughton
Cecile Niemitz-Rossant
Simon Srebrny
Roger Tebb